KU-712-531

edexcel
advancing learning, changing lives

BTEC National
Performing Arts

Study Guide

A PEARSON COMPANY

BTEC National Study Guide: Performing Arts

Published by:
Edexcel Limited
One90 High Holborn
London WC1V 7BH
www.edexcel.org.uk

Distributed by:
Pearson Education Limited
Edinburgh Gate
Harlow
Essex CM20 2JE

© Edexcel Limited 2007

All rights reserved. No part of this publication may be reproduced, stored in a retrieval system, or transmitted in any form
or by any means, electronic, mechanic, photocopying, recording, or otherwise without either the prior written permission
of the Publishers or a licence permitting restricted copying in the United Kingdom issued by the Copyright Licensing
Agency Ltd, 90 Tottenham Court Road, London W1P 9HE.

First published 2007

ISBN 978-1-84690-221-5

Project managed and typeset by Hart McLeod, Cambridge
Printed in Great Britain by Henry Ling Ltd., at the Dorset Press, Dorchester, Dorset

Cover image ©Paul Ridsdale/Alamy

The publisher's policy is to use paper manufactured from sustainable forests.

All reasonable efforts have been made to trace and contact original copyright owners.

This material offers high quality support for the delivery of Edexcel qualifications.
This does not mean that it is essential to achieve any Edexcel qualification, nor does it mean that this is the only suitable
material available to support any Edexcel qualification. No Edexcel-published material will be used verbatim in setting any
Edexcel assessment and any resource lists produced by Edexcel shall include this and other appropriate texts.

Acknowledgements

p.57 ©Michael Dinges/Photodisc/Getty Images; p.62 ©Emely/zefa/Corbis; p.66 ©Bloomimage/Corbis;
p.74 ©3D4Medical.com/Getty Images; p.79 ©Tom Merton/Digital Vision/Getty Images; p.81 ©James Leynse/Corbis;
p.85 ©Rob Barker; p.92 ©Andrew Holbrooke/Corbis; p.100 both ©Mary Evans Picture Library/Alamy

Contents

PREFACE

If you've already followed a BTEC First programme, you will know that this is an exciting way to study; if you are fresh from GCSEs you will find that from now on you will be in charge of your own learning. This guide has been written specially for you, to help get you started and then succeed on your BTEC National course.

The **Introduction** concentrates on making sure you have all the right facts about your course at your fingertips. Also, it guides you through the important skills you need to develop if you want to do well including:

- managing your time
- researching information
- preparing a presentation.

Keep this by your side throughout your course and dip into it whenever you need to.

The **Activities** give you tasks to do on your own, in a small group or as a class. They will help you internalise your learning and then prepare for assessment by practising your skills and showing you how much you know. These activities are not for assessment.

The sample **Assessed Assignments** show you what other students have done to gain Pass, Merit or Distinction. By seeing what past students have done, you should be able to improve your own grade.

Your BTEC National will cover six, twelve or eighteen units depending on whether you are doing an Award, Certificate or Diploma. In this guide the activities cover sections from Unit 3 – The Performing Arts Business, Unit 17 – Developing Voice for the Actor, Unit 20 – Applying Acting Styles and Unit 49 – Developing Movement Skills. These units underpin your study of Performing Arts.

Because the guide covers only four units, it is essential that you do all the other work your tutors set you. You will have to research information in textbooks, in the library and on the Internet. You should have the opportunity to visit local organisations and welcome visiting speakers to your institution. This is a great way to find out more about your chosen vocational area – the type of jobs that are available and what the work is really like.

This Guide is a taster, an introduction to your BTEC National. Use it as such and make the most of the rich learning environment that your tutors will provide for you. Your BTEC National will give you an excellent base for further study, a broad understanding of business and the knowledge you need to succeed in the world of work. Remember, thousands of students have achieved a BTEC National and are now studying for a degree or at work, building a successful career.

INTRODUCTION

SEVEN STEPS TO SUCCESS ON YOUR BTEC NATIONAL

You have received this guide because you have decided to do a BTEC National qualification. You may even have started your course. At this stage you should feel good about your decision. BTEC Nationals have many benefits – they are well-known and respected qualifications, they provide excellent preparation for future work or help you to get into university if that is your aim. If you are already at work then gaining a BTEC National will increase your value to your employer and help to prepare you for promotion.

Despite all these benefits though, you may be rather apprehensive about your ability to cope. Or you may be wildly enthusiastic about the whole course! More probably, you are somewhere between the two – perhaps quietly confident most of the time but sometimes worried that you may get out of your depth as the course progresses. You may be certain you made the right choice or still have days when your decision worries you. You may understand exactly what the course entails and what you have to do – or still feel rather bewildered, given all the new stuff you have to get your head around.

Your tutors will use the induction sessions at the start of your course to explain the important information they want you to know. At the time, though, it can be difficult to remember everything. This is especially true if you have just left school and are now studying in a new environment, among a group of people you have only just met. It is often only later that you think of useful questions to ask. Sometimes, misunderstandings or difficulties may only surface weeks or months into a course – and may continue for some time unless they are quickly resolved.

This student guide has been written to help to minimise these difficulties, so that you get the most out of your BTEC National course from day one. You can read through it at your own pace. You can look back at it whenever you have a problem or query.

This Introduction concentrates on making sure you have all the right facts about your course at your fingertips. This includes a **Glossary** (on page 32) which explains the specialist terms you may hear or read – including words and phrases highlighted in bold type in this Introduction.

The Introduction also guides you through the important skills you need to develop if you want to do well – such as managing your time, researching information and preparing a presentation; as well as reminding you about the key skills you will need to do justice to your work, such as good written and verbal communications.

Make sure you have all the right facts

5

- Use the PlusPoint boxes in each section to help you to stay focused on the essentials.

- Use the Action Point boxes to check out things you need to know or do right now.

- Refer to the Glossary (on page 32) if you need to check the meaning of any of the specialist terms you may hear or read.

Remember, thousands of students have achieved BTEC National Diplomas and are now studying for a degree or at work, building a successful career. Many were nervous and unsure of themselves at the outset – and very few experienced absolutely no setbacks during the course. What they did have, though, was a belief in their own ability to do well if they concentrated on getting things right one step at a time. This Introduction enables you to do exactly the same!

STEP ONE

UNDERSTAND YOUR COURSE AND HOW IT WORKS

What is a BTEC qualification and what does it involve? What will you be expected to do on the course? What can you do afterwards? How does this National differ from 'A' levels or a BTEC First qualification?

All these are common questions – but not all prospective students ask them! Did you? And, if so, did you really listen to the answers? And can you remember them now?

If you have already completed a BTEC First course then you may know some of the answers – although you may not appreciate some of the differences between that course and your new one.

Let's start by checking out the basics.

- All BTEC National qualifications are **vocational** or **work-related**. This doesn't mean that they give you all the skills that you need to do a job. It does mean that you gain the specific knowledge and understanding relevant to your chosen subject or area of work. This means that when you start in a job you will learn how to do the work more quickly and should progress further. If you are already employed, it means you become more valuable to your employer. You can choose to study a BTEC National in a wide range of vocational areas, such as Business, Health and Social Care, IT, Performing Arts and many others.

- There are three types of BTEC National qualification and each has a different number of units.

  - The BTEC National Award usually has 6 units and takes 360 **guided learning hours (GLH)** to complete. It is often offered as a part-time or short course but you may be one of the many students doing an Award alongside A-levels as a full-time course. An Award is equivalent to one 'A' level.

  - The BTEC National Certificate usually has 12 units and takes 720 GLH to complete. You may be able to study for the Certificate on a part-time or full-time course. It is equivalent to two 'A' levels.

– The BTEC National Diploma usually has 18 units and takes 1080 GLH to complete. It is normally offered as a two-year full-time course. It is equivalent to three 'A' levels.

These qualifications are often described as **nested**. This means that they fit inside each other (rather like Russian dolls!) because the same units are common to them all. This means that if you want to progress from one to another you can do so easily by simply completing more units.

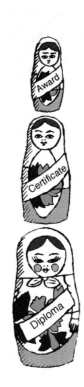

- Every BTEC National qualification has a set number of **core units**. These are the compulsory units every student must complete. The number of core units you will do on your course depends upon the vocational area you are studying.

- All BTEC National qualifications also have a range of **specialist units** from which you may be able to make a choice. These enable you to study particular areas in more depth.

- Some BTEC National qualifications have **specialist core units**. These are mandatory units you will have to complete if you want to follow a particular pathway in certain vocational areas. Engineering is an example of a qualification with the overarching title, Engineering, which has a set of core units that all students must complete. Then, depending what type of engineering a student wants to follow, there are more specialist core units that must be studied.

- On all BTEC courses you are expected to be in charge of your own learning. If you have completed a BTEC First, you will already have been introduced to this idea, but you can expect the situation to be rather different now that you are working at BTEC National level. Students on a BTEC First course will be expected to need more guidance whilst they develop their skills and find their feet. In some cases, this might last quite some time. On a BTEC National course you will be expected to take more responsibility for yourself and your own learning almost from the outset. You will quickly be expected to start thinking for yourself. This means planning what to do and carrying out a task without needing constant reminders. This doesn't mean that your tutor won't give you help and guidance when you need it. It does mean, though, that you need to be 'self-starting' and to be able to use your own initiative. You also need to be able to assess your own performance and make improvements when necessary. If you enjoy having the freedom to make your own decisions and work at your own pace then you will welcome this type of learning with open arms. However, there are dangers! If you are a procrastinator (look up this word if you don't know what it means!) then it's quite likely you will quickly get in a muddle. In this case read Step 3 – Use your time wisely – very carefully indeed!

- The way you are assessed and graded on a BTEC course is different from an 'A' level course, although you will still obtain UCAS points which you need if you want to go to university. You can read about this in the next section.

PLUSPOINTS

+ You can usually choose to study part-time or full-time for your BTEC National and do an Award, Certificate or Diploma and progress easily from one to the other.

+ You will study both core units and specialist units on your course.

+ When you have completed your BTEC course you can get a job (or **apprenticeship**), use your qualification to develop your career and/or continue your studies to degree level.

+ You are responsible for your own learning on a BTEC course. This prepares you for life at work or at university when you will be expected to be self-starting and to use your own initiative.

ACTION POINTS

✓ Check you know whether you are studying for an Award, Certificate or Diploma and find out the number of units you will be studying for your BTEC National qualification.

✓ Find out which are core and which are specialist units, and which specialist units are offered at your school or college.

✓ Check out the length of your course and when you will be studying each unit.

✓ Explore the Edexcel website at www.edexcel.org.uk. Your first task is to find what's available for your particular BTEC National qualification. Start by finding National qualifications, then look for your vocational area and check you are looking at the 2007 schemes. Then find the specification for your course. Don't print this out – it is far too long. You could, of course, save it if you want to refer to it regularly or you could just look through it for interest and then bookmark the pages relating to your qualification for future reference.

✓ Score yourself out of 5 (where 0 is awful and 5 is excellent) on each of the following to see how much improvement is needed for you to become responsible for your own learning!

Being punctual; organisational ability; tidiness; working accurately; finding and correcting own mistakes; solving problems; accepting responsibility; working with details; planning how to do a job; using own initiative; thinking up new ideas; meeting deadlines.

✓ Draw up your own action plan to improve any areas where you are weak. Talk this through at your next individual **tutorial**.

STEP TWO

UNDERSTAND HOW YOU ARE ASSESSED AND GRADED – AND USE THIS KNOWLEDGE TO YOUR ADVANTAGE!

If you already have a BTEC First qualification, you may think that you don't need to read this section because you assume that BTEC National is simply more of the same. Whilst there are some broad similarities, you will now be working at an entirely different level and the grades you get for your work could be absolutely crucial to your future plans.

Equally, if you have opted for BTEC National rather than 'A' level because you thought you would have less work (or writing) to do then you need to read this section very carefully. Indeed, if you chose your BTEC National because you thought it would guarantee you an easy life, you are likely to get quite a shock when reality hits home!

It is true that, unlike 'A' levels, there are no exams on a BTEC course. However, to do well you need to understand the importance of your assignments, how these are graded and how these convert into unit points and UCAS points. This is the focus of this section.

Your assignments

On a BTEC National course your learning is assessed by means of **assignments** set by your tutors and given to you to complete throughout your course.

- Your tutors will use a variety of **assessment methods**, such as case studies, projects, presentations and shows to obtain evidence of your skills and knowledge to date. You may also be given work-based or **time-constrained** assignments – where your performance might be observed and assessed. It will depend very much on the vocational area you are studying (see also page 16).

- Important skills you will need to learn are how to research information (see page 25) and how to use your time effectively, particularly if you have to cope with several assignments at the same time (see page 12). You may also be expected to work cooperatively as a member of a team to complete some parts of your assignments – especially if you are doing a subject like Performing Arts – or to prepare a presentation (see page 26).

- All your assignments are based on **learning outcomes** set by Edexcel. These are listed for each unit in your course specification. You have to meet *all* the learning outcomes to pass the unit.

Your grades

On a BTEC National course, assignments that meet the learning outcomes are graded as Pass, Merit or Distinction.

- The difference between these grades has very little to do with how much you write! Edexcel sets out the **grading criteria** for the different grades in a **grading grid**. This identifies the **higher-level skills** you have to demonstrate to earn a higher grade. You can find out more about this, and read examples of good (and not so good) answers to assignments at Pass, Merit and Distinction level in the assessed assignments section starting on page 103. You will also find out more about getting the best grade you can in Step 5 – Understand your assessment – on page 16.

- Your grades for all your assignments earn you **unit points**. The number of points you get for each unit is added together and your total score determines your final grade(s) for the qualification – again either Pass, Merit or Distinction. You get one final grade if you are taking a BTEC National Award, two if you are taking a BTEC National Certificate and three if you are taking a BTEC National Diploma.

- Your points and overall grade(s) also convert to **UCAS points** which you will need if you want to apply to study on a degree course. As an example, if you are studying a BTEC National Diploma, and achieve three final pass grades you will achieve 120 UCAS points. If you achieve three final distinction grades the number of UCAS points you have earned goes up to 360.

- It is important to note that you start earning both unit and UCAS points from the very first assignment you complete! This means that if you take a long time to settle into your course, or to start working productively, you could easily lose valuable points for quite some time. If you have your heart set on a particular university or degree course then this could limit your choices. Whichever way you look at it, it is silly to squander potentially good grades for an assignment and their equivalent points, just because you didn't really understand what you had to do – which is why this guide has been written to help you!

- If you take a little time to understand how **grade boundaries** work, you can see where you need to concentrate your efforts to get the best final grade possible. Let's give a simple example. Chris and Shaheeda both want to go to university and have worked hard on their BTEC National Diploma course. Chris ends with a total score of 226 unit points which converts to 280 UCAS points. Shaheeda ends with a total score of 228 unit points – just two points more – which converts to 320 UCAS points! This is because a score of between 204 and 227 unit points gives 280 UCAS points, whereas a score of 228 – 251 points gives 320 UCAS points. Shaheeda is pleased because this increases her chances of getting a place on the degree course she wants. Chris is annoyed. He says if he had known then he would have put more effort into his last assignment to get two points more.

- It is always tempting to spend time on work you like doing, rather than work you don't – but this can be a mistake if you have already done the best you can at an assignment and it would already earn a very good grade. Instead you should now concentrate on improving an assignment which covers an area where you know you are weak, because this will boost your overall grade(s). You will learn more about this in Step 3 – Use your time wisely.

PLUSPOINTS

+ Your learning is assessed in a variety of ways, such as by assignments, projects and case studies. You will need to be able to research effectively, manage your own time and work well with other people to succeed.

+ You need to demonstrate specific knowledge and skills to achieve the learning outcomes set by Edexcel. You need to demonstrate you can meet all the learning outcomes to pass a unit.

+ Higher-level skills are required for higher grades. The grading criteria for Pass, Merit and Distinction grades are set out in a grading grid for the unit.

+ The assessment grades of Pass, Merit and Distinction convert to unit points. The total number of unit points you receive during the course determines your final overall grade(s) and the UCAS points you have earned.

+ Working effectively from the beginning maximises your chances of achieving a good qualification grade. Understanding grade boundaries enables you to get the best final grade(s) possible.

ACTION POINTS

✓ Find the learning outcomes for the units you are currently studying. Your tutor may have given you these already, or you can find them in the specification for your course that you already accessed at www.edexcel.org.uk.

✓ Look at the grading grid for the units and identify the way the evidence required changes to achieve the higher grades. Don't worry if there are some words that you do not understand – these are explained in more detail on page 32 of this guide.

✓ If you are still unsure how the unit points system works, ask your tutor to explain it to you.

✓ Check out the number of UCAS points you would need for any course or university in which you are interested.

✓ Keep a record of the unit points you earn throughout your course and check regularly how this is affecting your overall grade(s), based on the grade boundaries for your qualification. Your tutor will give you this information or you can check it yourself in the specification for your course on the Edexcel website.

STEP THREE

USE YOUR TIME WISELY

Most students on a BTEC National course are trying to combine their course commitments with a number of others – such as a job (either full or part-time) and family responsibilities. In addition, they still want time to meet with friends, enjoy a social life and keep up hobbies and interests that they have.

Starting the course doesn't mean that you have to hide away for months if you want to do well. It does mean that you have to use your time wisely if you want to do well, stay sane and keep a balance in your life.

You will only do this if you make time work for you, rather than against you, by taking control. This means that you decide what you are doing, when you are doing it and work purposefully; rather than simply reacting to problems or panicking madly because you've yet another deadline staring you in the face.

Use your time wisely

This becomes even more important as your course progresses because your workload is likely to increase, particularly towards the end of a term. In the early days you may be beautifully organised and able to cope easily. Then you may find you have several tasks to complete simultaneously as well as some research to start. Then you get two assignments in the same week from different tutors – as well as having a presentation to prepare. Then another assignment is scheduled for the following week – and so on. This is not because your tutors are being deliberately difficult. Indeed, most will try to schedule your assignments to avoid such clashes. The problem, of course, is that none of your tutors can assess your abilities until you have learned something – so if several units start and end at the same time it is highly likely there will be some overlap between your assignments.

To cope when the going gets tough, without collapsing into an exhausted heap, you need to learn a few time management skills.

- **Pinpoint where your time goes at the moment** Time is like money – it's usually difficult to work out where it all went! Work out how much time you currently spend at college, at work, at home and on social activities. Check, too, how much time you waste each week – and why this happens. Are you disorganised or do you easily get distracted? Then identify commitments that are vital and those that are optional so that you know where you can find time if you need to.

- **Plan when and where to work** It is unrealistic not to expect to do quite a lot of work for your course in your own time. It is also better to work regularly, and in relatively short bursts, than to work just once or twice a week for very long stretches. In addition to deciding when to work, and for how long, you also need to think about when and where to work. If you are a lark, you will work better early in the day; if you are an owl, you will be at your best later on. Whatever time you work, you need somewhere quiet so that you can concentrate and with space for books and other resources you need. If the words 'quiet oasis' and 'your house' are totally incompatible at any time of the day or night then check out the opening hours of your local and college library so that you have an escape route if you need it. If you are trying to combine studying with parental responsibilities it is sensible to factor in your children's commitments – and work around their bedtimes too! Store up favours, too, from friends and grandparents that you can call in if you get desperate for extra time when an assignment deadline is looming.

- **Schedule your commitments** Keep a diary or (even better) a wall chart and write down every appointment you make or task you are given. It is useful to use a colour code to differentiate between personal and work or course commitments. You may also want to enter assignment review dates with your tutor in one colour and final deadline dates in another. Keep your diary or chart up-to-date by adding any new dates promptly every time you receive another task or assignment or whenever you make any other arrangements. Keep checking ahead so that you always have prior warning when important dates are looming. This stops you from planning a heavy social week when you will be at your busiest at work or college and from arranging a dental appointment on the morning when you and your team are scheduled to give an important presentation!

- **Prioritise your work** This means doing the most important and urgent task first, rather than the one you like the most! Normally this will be the task or assignment with the nearest deadline. There are two exceptions. Sometimes you may need to send off for information and allow time for it to arrive. It is therefore sensible to do this first so that you are not held up later. The second is when you have to take account of other people's schedules – because you are working in a team or are arranging to interview someone, for example. In this case you will have to arrange your schedule around their needs, not just your own.

- **Set sensible timescales** Trying to do work at the last minute or in a rush is never satisfactory, so it is wise always to allocate more time than you think you will need, never less. Remember, too, to include all the stages of a complex task or assignment, such as researching the information, deciding what to use, creating a first draft, checking it and making improvements and printing it out. If you are planning to do any of your work in a central facility always allow extra time and try to start work early. If you arrive at the last minute you may find every computer and printer is fully utilised until closing time.

- **Learn self-discipline!** This means not putting things off (procrastinating!) because you don't know where to start or don't feel in the mood. Unless you are ill, you have to find some way of persuading yourself to work. One way is to bribe yourself. Make a start and promise yourself that if you work productively for 30 minutes then you deserve a small reward. After 30 minutes you may have become more engrossed and want to keep going a little longer. Otherwise at least you have made a start, so it's easier to come back and do more later. It doesn't matter whether you have research to do, an assignment to write up, a coaching session to plan, or lines to learn, you need to be self-disciplined.

- **Take regular breaks and keep your life in balance** Don't go to the opposite extreme and work for hours on end. Take regular breaks to give yourself a rest and a change of activity. You need to recharge your batteries! Similarly, don't cancel every social arrangement so that you can work 24/7. Whilst this may be occasionally necessary if you have several deadlines looming simultaneously, it should only be a last resort. If you find yourself doing this regularly then go back to the beginning of this section and see where your time–management planning is going wrong.

PLUSPOINTS

+ Being in control of your time enables you to balance your commitments according to their importance and allows you not let to anyone down – including yourself.

+ Controlling time involves knowing how you spend (and waste!) your time now, planning when best to do work, scheduling your commitments and setting sensible timescales for work to be done.

+ Knowing how to prioritise means that you will schedule work effectively according to its urgency and importance but this also requires self-discipline. You have to follow the schedule you have set for yourself!

+ Managing time and focusing on the task at hand means you will do better work and be less stressed, because you are not having to react to problems or crises. You can also find the time to include regular breaks and leisure activities in your schedule.

ACTION POINTS

✓ Find out how many assignments you can expect to receive this term and when you can expect to receive these. Enter this information into your student diary or onto a planner you can refer to regularly.

✓ Update your diary and/or planner with other commitments that you have this term – both work/college-related and social. Identify any potential clashes and decide the best action to take to solve the problem.

✓ Identify your own best time and place to work quietly and effectively.

✓ Displacement activities are things we do to put off starting a job we don't want to do – such as sending texts, watching TV, checking emails etc. Identify yours so that you know when you're doing them!

STEP FOUR

UTILISE ALL YOUR RESOURCES

Your resources are all the things that can help you to achieve your qualification. They can therefore be as wide-ranging as your favourite website and your **study buddy** (see below) who collects handouts for you if you miss a class.

Your college will provide the essential resources for your course, such as a library with a wide range of books and electronic reference sources, learning resource centre(s), the computer network and Internet access. Other basic resources you will be expected to provide yourself, such as file folders and paper. The policy on textbooks varies from one college to another, but on most courses today students are expected to buy their own. If you look after yours carefully, then you have the option to sell it on to someone else afterwards and recoup some of your money. If you scribble all over it, leave it on the floor and then tread on it, turn back pages and rapidly turn it into a dog-eared, misshapen version of its former self then you miss out on this opportunity.

Unfortunately students often squander other opportunities to utilise resources in the best way – usually because they don't think about them very much, if at all. To help, below is a list of the resources you should consider important – with a few tips on how to get the best out of them.

- **Course information** This includes your course specification, this Study Guide and all the other information relating to your BTEC National which you can find on the Edexcel website. Add to this all the information given to you at college relating to your course, including term dates, assignment dates and, of course, your timetable. This should not be 'dead' information that you glance at once and then discard or ignore. Rather it is important reference material that you need to store somewhere obvious, so that you can look at it whenever you have a query or need to clarify something quickly.

- **Course materials** In this group is your textbook (if there is one), the handouts you are given as well as print-outs and notes you make yourself. File handouts the moment you are given them and put them into an A4 folder bought for the purpose. You will need one for each unit you study. Some students prefer lever-arch files but these are more bulky so more difficult to carry around all day. Unless you have a locker at college it can be easier to keep a lever arch file at home for permanent storage of past handouts and notes for a unit and carry an A4 folder with you which contains current topic information. Filing handouts and print-outs promptly means they don't get lost. They are also less likely to get crumpled, torn or tatty becoming virtually unreadable. Unless you have a private and extensive source of income then this is even more important if you have to pay for every print-out you take in your college resource centre. If you are following a course such as Art and Design, then there will be all your art materials and the pieces you produce. You must look after these with great care.

- **Other stationery items** Having your own pens, pencils, notepad, punch, stapler and sets of dividers is essential. Nothing irritates tutors more than watching one punch circulate around a group – except, perhaps, the student who trudges into class with nothing to write on or with. Your dividers should be clearly labelled to help you store and find notes, print-outs and handouts fast. Similarly, your notes should be clearly headed and dated. If you are writing notes up from your own research then you will have to include your source. Researching information is explained in Step 6 – Sharpen your skills.

- **Equipment and facilities** These include your college library and resource centres, the college computer network and other college equipment you can use, such as laptop computers, photocopiers and presentation equipment. Much of this may be freely available; others – such as using the photocopier in the college library or the printers in a resource centre – may cost you money. Many useful resources will be electronic, such as DVDs or electronic journals and databases. At home you may have your own computer with Internet access to count as a resource. Finally, include any specialist equipment and facilities available for your particular course that you use at college or have at home.

Utilise all your resources

All centralised college resources and facilities are invaluable if you know how to use them – but can be baffling when you don't. Your induction should have included how to use the library, resource centre(s) and computer network. You should also have been informed of the policy on using IT equipment which determines what you can and can't do when you are using college computers. If, by any chance, you missed this then go and check it out for yourself. Library and resource centre staff will be only too pleased to give you helpful advice – especially if you pick a quiet time to call in. You can also find out about the allowable ways to transfer data between your college computer and your home computer if your options are limited because of IT security.

Having a study buddy is a good idea

- **People** You are surrounded by people who are valuable resources: your tutor(s), specialist staff at college, your employer and work colleagues, your relatives and any friends who have particular skills or who work in the same area you are studying. Other members of your class are also useful resources – although they may not always seem like it! Use them, for example, to discuss topics out of class time. A good debate between a group of students can often raise and clarify issues that there may not be time to discuss fully in class. Having a study buddy is another good idea – you get/make notes for them when they are away and vice versa. That way you don't miss anything.

  If you want information or help from someone, especially anyone outside your immediate circle, then remember to get the basics right! Approach them courteously, do your homework first so that you are well-prepared and remember that you are asking for assistance – not trying to get them to do the work for you! If someone has agreed to allow you to interview them as part of your research for an assignment or project then good preparations will be vital, as you will see in Step 6 – Sharpen your Skills (see page 22).

  One word of warning: be wary about using information from friends or relatives who have done a similar or earlier course. First, the slant of the material they were given may be different. It may also be out-of-date. And *never* copy anyone else's written assignments. This is **plagiarism** – a deadly sin in the educational world. You can read more about this in Step 5 – Understand your assessment (see page 16).

- **You!** You have the ability to be your own best resource or your own worst enemy! The difference depends upon your work skills, your personal skills and your attitude to your course and other people. You have already seen how to use time wisely. Throughout this guide you will find out how to sharpen and improve other work and personal skills and how to get the most out of your course – but it is up to you to read it and apply your new-found knowledge! This is why attributes like a positive attitude, an enquiring mind and the ability to focus on what is important all have a major impact on your final result.

15

PLUSPOINTS

+ Resources help you to achieve your qualification. You will squander these unwittingly if you don't know what they are or how to use them properly.

+ Course information needs to be stored safely for future reference: course materials need to be filed promptly and accurately so that you can find them quickly.

+ You need your own set of key stationery items; you also need to know how to use any central facilities or resources such as the library, learning resource centres and your computer network.

+ People are often a key resource – school or college staff, work colleagues, members of your class, people who are experts in their field.

+ You can be your own best resource! Develop the skills you need to be able to work quickly and accurately and to get the most out of other people who can help you.

ACTION POINTS

✓ Under the same headings as in this section, list all the resources you need for your course and tick off those you currently have. Then decide how and when you can obtain anything vital that you lack.

✓ Check that you know how to access and use all the shared resources to which you have access at school or college.

✓ Pair up with someone on your course as a study buddy – and don't let them down!

✓ Test your own storage systems. How fast can you find notes or print-outs you made yesterday/last week/last month – and what condition are they in?

✓ Find out the IT policy at your school or college and make sure you abide by it.

STEP FIVE

UNDERSTAND YOUR ASSESSMENT

The key to doing really, really well on any BTEC National course is to understand exactly what you are expected to do in your assignments – and then to do it! It really is as simple as that. So why is it that some people go wrong?

Obviously you may worry that an assignment may be so difficult that it is beyond you. Actually this is highly unlikely to happen because all your assignments are based on topics you will have already covered thoroughly in class. Therefore, if you have attended regularly – and have clarified any queries or worries you have either in class or during your tutorials – this shouldn't happen. If you have had an unavoidable lengthy absence then you may need to review your progress with your tutor and decide how best to cope with the situation. Otherwise, you should note that the main problems with assignments are usually due to far more mundane pitfalls – such as:

✗ not reading the instructions or the assignment brief properly

✗ not understanding what you are supposed to do

✗ only doing part of the task or answering part of a question

✗ skimping the preparation, the research or the whole thing

✗ not communicating your ideas clearly

✗ guessing answers rather than researching properly

✗ padding out answers with irrelevant information

✗ leaving the work until the last minute and then doing it in a rush

✗ ignoring advice and feedback your tutor has given you.

You can avoid all of these traps by following the guidelines below so that you know exactly what you are doing, prepare well and produce your best work.

The assignment 'brief'

The word 'brief' is just another way of saying 'instructions'. Often, though, a 'brief' (despite its name!) may be rather longer. The brief sets the context for the work, defines what evidence you will need to produce and matches the grading criteria to the tasks. It will also give you a schedule for completing the tasks. For example, a brief may include details of a case study you have to read; research you have to carry out or a task you have to do, as well as questions you have to answer. Or it may give you details about a project or group presentation you have to prepare. The type of assignments you receive will depend partly upon the vocational area you are studying, but you can expect some to be in the form of written assignments. Others are likely to be more practical or project-based, especially if you are doing a very practical subject such as Art and Design, Performing Arts or Sport. You may also be assessed in the workplace. For example, this is a course requirement if you are studying Children's Care, Learning and Development.

The assignment brief may also include the **learning outcomes** to which it relates. These tell you the purpose of the assessment and the knowledge you need to demonstrate to obtain a required grade. If your brief doesn't list the learning outcomes, then you should check this information against the unit specification to see the exact knowledge you need to demonstrate.

The grade(s) you can obtain will also be stated on the assignment brief. Sometimes an assignment will focus on just one grade. Others may give you the opportunity to develop or extend your work to progress to a higher grade. This is often dependent upon submitting acceptable work at the previous grade first. You will see examples of this in the Marked Assignment section of this Study Guide on page 103.

The brief will also tell you if you have to do part of the work as a member of a group. In this case, you must identify your own contribution. You may also be expected to take part in a **peer review**, where you all give feedback on the contribution of one another. Remember that you should do this as objectively and professionally as possible – not just praise everyone madly in the hope that they will do the same for you! In any assignment where there is a group contribution, there is virtually always an individual component, so that your individual grade can be assessed accurately.

Finally, your assignment brief should state the final deadline for handing in the work as well as any interim review dates when you can discuss your progress and ideas with your tutor. These are very important dates indeed and should be entered immediately into your diary or planner. You should schedule your work around these dates so that you have made a start by the first date. This will then enable you to note any queries or significant issues you want to discuss. Otherwise you will waste a valuable opportunity to obtain useful feedback on your progress. Remember, too, to take a notebook to any review meetings so that you can write down the guidance you are given.

Your school or college rules and regulations

Your school or college will have a number of policies and guidelines about assignments and assessment. These will deal with issues such as:

- The procedure you must follow if you have a serious personal problem so cannot meet the deadline date and need an extension.
- Any penalties for missing a deadline date without any good reason.
- The penalties for copying someone else's work (**plagiarism**). These will be severe so make sure that you never share your work (including your CDs) with anyone else and don't ask to borrow theirs.
- The procedure to follow if you are unhappy with the final grade you receive.

Even though it is unlikely that you will ever need to use any of these policies, it is sensible to know they exist, and what they say, just as a safeguard.

Understanding the question or task

There are two aspects to a question or task that need attention. The first are the *command words*, which are explained below. The second are the *presentation instructions*, so that if you are asked to produce a table or graph or report then you do exactly that – and don't write a list or an essay instead!

Command words are used to specify how a question must be answered, eg 'explain', 'describe', 'analyse', 'evaluate'. These words relate to the type of answer required. So whereas you may be asked to 'describe' something at Pass level, you will need to do more (such as 'analyse' or 'evaluate') to achieve Merit or Distinction grade.

Many students fail to get a higher grade because they do not realise the difference between these words. They simply don't know *how* to analyse or evaluate, so give an explanation instead. Just adding to a list or giving a few more details will never give you a higher grade – instead you need to change your whole approach to the answer.

The **grading grid** for each unit of your course gives you the command words, so that you can find out exactly what you have to do in each unit, to obtain a Pass, Merit and Distinction. The following charts show you what is usually required when you see a particular command word. You can use this, and the assessed assignments on pages 103–182, to see the difference between the types of answers required for each grade. (The assignments your centre gives you will be specially written to ensure you have the opportunity to achieve all the possible grades.) Remember, though, that these are just examples to guide you. The exact response will often depend upon the way a question is worded, so if you have any doubts at all check with your tutor before you start work.

There are two other important points to note:

- Sometimes the same command word may be repeated for different grades – such as 'create' or 'explain'. In this case the *complexity* or *range* of the task itself increases at the higher grades – as you will see if you read the grading grid for the unit.

- Command words can also vary depending upon your vocational area. If you are studying Performing Arts or Art and Design you will probably find several command words that an Engineer or IT Practitioner would not – and vice versa!

To obtain a Pass grade

To achieve this grade you must usually demonstrate that you understand the important facts relating to a topic and can state these clearly and concisely.

Command word	What this means
Create (or produce)	Make, invent or construct an item.
Describe	Give a clear, straightforward description that includes all the main points and links these together logically.
Define	Clearly explain what a particular term means and give an example, if appropriate, to show what you mean.
Explain . . . how/why	Set out in detail the meaning of something, with reasons. It is often helpful to give an example of what you mean. Start with the topic then give the 'how' or 'why'.
Identify	Distinguish and state the main features or basic facts relating to a topic.
Interpret	Define or explain the meaning of something.
Illustrate	Give examples to show what you mean.
List	Provide the information required in a list rather than in continuous writing.
Outline	Write a clear description that includes all the main points but avoid going into too much detail.
Plan (or devise)	Work out and explain how you would carry out a task or activity.
Select (and present) information	Identify relevant information to support the argument you are making and communicate this in an appropriate way.
State	Write a clear and full account.
Undertake	Carry out a specific activity.
Examples: **Identify** the main features on a digital camera. **Describe** your usual lifestyle. **Outline** the steps to take to carry out research for an assignment.	

To obtain a Merit grade

To obtain this grade you must prove that you can apply your knowledge in
a specific way.

Command word	What this means
Analyse	Identify separate factors, say how they are related and how each one relates to the topic.
Classify	Sort your information into appropriate categories before presenting or explaining it.
Compare and contrast	Identify the main factors that apply in two or more situations and explain the similarities and differences or advantages and disadvantages.
Demonstrate	Provide several relevant examples or appropriate evidence which support the arguments you are making. In some vocational areas this may also mean giving a practical performance.
Discuss	Provide a thoughtful and logical argument to support the case you are making.
Explain (in detail)	Provide details and give reasons and/or evidence to clearly support the argument you are making.
Implement	Put into practice or operation. You may also have to interpret or justify the effect or result.
Interpret	Understand and explain an effect or result.
Justify	Give appropriate reasons to support your opinion or views and show how you arrived at these conclusions.
Relate/report	Give a full account of, with reasons.
Research	Carry out a full investigation.
Specify	Provide full details and descriptions of selected items or activities.
Examples:	

Examples:

Compare and contrast the performance of two different digital cameras.
Justify your usual lifestyle.
Explain in detail the steps to take to research an assignment.

To obtain a Distinction grade

To obtain this grade you must prove that you can make a reasoned judgement based on appropriate evidence.

Command word	What this means
Analyse	Identify the key factors, show how they are linked and explain the importance and relevance of each.
Assess	Give careful consideration to all the factors or events that apply and identify which are the most important and relevant with reasons for your views.
Comprehensively explain	Give a very detailed explanation that covers all the relevant points and give reasons for your views or actions.
Comment critically	Give your view after you have considered all the evidence, particularly the importance of both the relevant positive and negative aspects.
Evaluate	Review the information and then bring it together to form a conclusion. Give evidence to support each of your views or statements.
Evaluate critically	Review the information to decide the degree to which something is true, important or valuable. Then assess possible alternatives taking into account their strengths and weaknesses if they were applied instead. Then give a precise and detailed account to explain your opinion.
Summarise	Identify and review the main, relevant factors and/or arguments so that these are explained in a clear and concise manner.
Examples: **Assess** ten features commonly found on a digital camera. **Evaluate critically** your usual lifestyle. **Analyse** your own ability to carry out effective research for an assignment.	

Responding positively

This is often the most important attribute of all! If you believe that assignments give you the opportunity to demonstrate what you know and how you can apply it *and* positively respond to the challenge by being determined to give it your best shot, then you will do far better than someone who is defeated before they start.

It obviously helps, too, if you are well organised and have confidence in your own abilities – which is what the next section is all about!

PLUSPOINTS

+ Many mistakes in assignments are through errors that can easily be avoided such as not reading the instructions properly or doing only part of the task that was set!

+ Always read the assignment brief very carefully indeed. Check that you understand exactly what you have to do and the learning outcomes you must demonstrate.

+ Make a note of the deadline for an assignment and any interim review dates on your planner. Schedule work around these dates so that you can make the most of reviews with your tutor.

+ Make sure you know about school or college policies relating to assessment, such as how to obtain an extension or query a final grade.

+ For every assignment, make sure you understand the command words, which tell you how to answer the question, and the presentation instructions, which say what you must produce.

+ Command words are shown in the grading grid for each unit of your qualification. Expect command words and/or the complexity of a task to be different at higher grades, because you have to demonstrate higher-level skills.

ACTION POINTS

✓ Discuss with your tutor the format (style) of assignments you are likely to receive on your course, eg assignments, projects, or practical work where you are observed.

✓ Check the format of the assignments in the Assessed Assignments section of this book. Look at the type of work students did to gain a Pass and then look at the difference in the Merit answers. Read the tutor's comments carefully and ask your own tutor if there is anything you do not understand.

✓ Check out all the policies and guidelines at your school or college that relate to assessment and make sure you understand them.

✓ Check out the grading grid for the units you are currently studying and identify the command words for each grade. Then check you understand what they mean using the explanations above. If there are any words that are not included, ask your tutor to explain the meanings and what you would be required to do.

STEP SIX

SHARPEN YOUR SKILLS

To do your best in any assignment you need a number of skills. Some of these may be vocationally specific, or professional, skills that you are learning as part of your course – such as acting or dancing if you are taking a Performing Arts course or, perhaps, football if you are following a Sports course. Others, though, are broader skills that will help you to do well in assignments no matter what subjects or topics you are studying – such as communicating clearly and cooperating with others.

Some of these skills you will have already and in some areas you may be extremely proficient. Knowing where your weaknesses lie, though, and doing something about them has many benefits. You will work more quickly, more accurately *and* have increased confidence in your own abilities. As an extra bonus, all these skills also make you more effective at work – so there really is no excuse for not giving yourself a quick skills check and then remedying any problem areas.

This section contains hints and tips to help you check out and improve each of the following areas:

- Your numeracy skills
- Keyboarding and document preparation
- Your IT skills
- Your written communication skills
- Working with others
- Researching information
- Making a presentation

Your numeracy skills

Some people have the idea that they can ignore numeracy because this skill isn't relevant to their vocational area – such as Art and Design or Children's Care, Learning and Development. If this is how you think then you are wrong! Numeracy is a life skill that everyone needs, so if you can't carry out basic calculations accurately then you will have problems, often when you least expect them.

Fortunately there are several things you can do to remedy this situation:

- Practise basic calculations in your head and then check them on a calculator.
- Ask your tutor if there are any essential calculations which give you difficulties.
- Use your onscreen calculator (or a spreadsheet package) to do calculations for you when you are using your computer.
- Try your hand at Sudoku puzzles – either on paper or by using a software package or online at sites such as www.websudoku.com/.
- Investigate puzzle sites and brain training software, such as http://school.discovery.com/brainboosters/ and Dr Kawashima's Brain Training by Nintendo.
- Check out online sites such as www.bbc.co.uk/skillswise/ and www.bbc.co.uk/schools/ks3bitesize/maths/number/index.shtml to improve your skills.

Numeracy is a life skill

Keyboarding and document preparation

- Think seriously about learning to touch type to save hours of time! Your school or college may have a workshop you can join or you can learn online such as by downloading a free program at www.sense-lang.org/typing/ or practising on sites such as www.computerlab.kids.new.net/keyboarding.htm.
- Obtain correct examples of document formats you will have to use, such as a report or summary. Your tutor may provide you with these or you can find examples in many communication textbooks.
- Proofread work you produce on a computer *carefully*. Remember that your spell checker will not pick up every mistake you make, such as a mistyped word that makes another word (eg form/from; sheer/shear)

23

and grammar checkers, too, are not without their problems! This means you still have to read your work through yourself. If possible, let your work go 'cold' before you do this so that you read it afresh and don't make assumptions about what you have written. Then read word by word to make sure it still makes sense and there are no silly mistakes, such as missing or duplicated words.

- Make sure your work looks professional by using an appropriate typeface and font size as well as suitable margins.
- Print out your work carefully and store it neatly, so it looks in pristine condition when you hand it in.

Your IT skills

- Check that you can use the main features of all the software packages that you will need to produce your assignments, such as Word, Excel and PowerPoint.
- Adopt a good search engine, such as Google, and learn to use it properly. Many have online tutorials such as www.googleguide.com.
- Develop your IT skills to enable you to enhance your assignments appropriately. For example, this may include learning how to import and export text and artwork from one package to another; taking digital photographs and inserting them into your work and/or creating drawings or diagrams by using appropriate software for your course.

Your written communication skills

A poor vocabulary will reduce your ability to explain yourself clearly; work peppered with spelling or punctuation errors looks unprofessional.

- Read more. This introduces you to new words and familiarises you over and over again with the correct way to spell words.
- Look up words you don't understand in a dictionary and then try to use them yourself in conversation.
- Use the Thesaurus in Word to find alternatives to words you find yourself regularly repeating, to add variety to your work.
- *Never* use words you don't understand in the hope that they sound impressive!
- Do crosswords to improve your word power and spelling.
- Resolve to master punctuation – especially apostrophes – either by using an online programme or working your way through the relevant section of a communication textbook that you like.
- Check out online sites such as www.bbc.co.uk/skillswise/ and www.bbc.co.uk/schools/gcsebitesize/english/ as well as puzzle sites with communication questions such as http://school.discovery.com/brainboosters/.

Working with others

In your private life you can choose who you want to be with and how you respond to them. At work you cannot do that – you are paid to be professional and this means working alongside a wide variety of people, some of whom you may like and some of whom you may not!

The same applies at school or college. By the time you have reached BTEC National level you will be expected to have outgrown wanting to work with your best friends on every project! You may not be very keen on everyone who is in the same team as you, but – at the very least – you can be pleasant, cooperative and helpful. In a large group this isn't normally too difficult. You may find it much harder if you have to partner someone who has very different ideas and ways of working to you.

In this case it may help if you:

- Realise that everyone is different and that your ways of working may not always be the best!
- Are prepared to listen and contribute to a discussion (positively) in equal amounts. Make sure, too, that you encourage the quiet members of the group to speak up by asking them what their views are. The ability to draw other people into the discussion is an important and valuable skill to learn.
- Write down what you have said you will do, so that you don't forget anything.
- Are prepared to do your fair share of the work.
- Discuss options and alternatives with people – don't give them orders or meekly accept instructions and then resent it afterwards.
- Don't expect other people to do what you wouldn't be prepared to do.
- Are sensitive to other people's feelings and remember that they may have personal problems or issues that affect their behaviour.
- *Always* keep your promises and never let anyone down when they are depending upon you.
- Don't flounce around or lose your temper if things get tough. Instead take a break while you cool down. Then sit down and discuss the issues that are annoying you.
- Help other people to reach a compromise when necessary, by acting as peacemaker.

Researching information

Poor researchers either cannot find what they want or find too much – and then drown in a pile of papers. If you find yourself drifting aimlessly around a library when you want information or printing out dozens of pages for no apparent purpose, then this section is for you!

- Always check *exactly* what it is you need to find and how much detail is needed. Write down a few key words to keep yourself focused.
- Discipline yourself to ignore anything that is irrelevant – from books with interesting titles to websites which sound tempting but have little to do with your topic or key words.
- Remember that you could theoretically research information forever! So at some time you have to call a halt. Learning when to do this is another skill, but you can learn this by writing out a schedule which clearly states when you have to stop looking and start sorting out your information and writing about it!

- In a library, check you know how the books are stored and what other types of media are available. If you can't find what you are looking for then ask the librarian for help. Checking the index in a book is the quickest way to find out whether it contains information related to your key words. Put it back if it doesn't or if you can't understand it. If you find three or four books and/or journals that contain what you need then that is usually enough.

- Online use a good search engine and use the summary of the search results to check out the best sites. Force yourself to check out sites beyond page one of the search results! When you enter a site investigate it carefully – use the site map if necessary. It isn't always easy to find exactly what you want. Bookmark sites you find helpful and will want to use again and only take print-outs when the information is closely related to your key words.

- Talk to people who can help you (see also Step 4 – Utilise all your resources) and prepare in advance by thinking about the best questions to ask. Always explain why you want the information and don't expect anyone to tell you anything that is confidential or sensitive – such as personal information or financial details. Always write clear notes so that you remember what you have been told, by whom and when. If you are wise you will also note down their contact details so that you can contact them again if you think of anything later. If you remember to be courteous and thank them for their help, this shouldn't be a problem.

- Store all your precious information carefully and neatly in a labelled folder so that you can find it easily. Then, when you are ready to start work, reread it and extract that which is most closely related to your key words and the task you are doing.

- Make sure you state the source of all the information you quote by including the name of the author or the web address, either in the text or as part of a bibliography at the end. Your school or college will have a help sheet which will tell you exactly how to do this.

Making a presentation

This involves several skills – which is why it is such a popular way of finding out what students can do! It will test your ability to work in a team, speak in public and use IT (normally PowerPoint) – as well as your nerves. It is therefore excellent practice for many of the tasks you will have to do when you are at work – from attending an interview to talking to an important client.

You will be less nervous if you have prepared well and have rehearsed your role beforehand. You will produce a better, more professional presentation if you take note of the following points.

- If you are working as a team, work out everyone's strengths and weaknesses and divide up the work (fairly) taking these into account. Work out, too, how long each person should speak and who would be the best as the 'leader' who introduces each person and then summarises everything at the end.

PLUSPOINTS

+ Poor numeracy skills can let you down in your assignments and at work. Work at improving these if you regularly struggle with even simple calculations.

+ Good keyboarding, document production and IT skills can save you hours of time and mean that your work is of a far more professional standard. Improve any of these areas which are letting you down.

+ Your written communication skills will be tested in many assignments. Work at improving areas of weakness, such as spelling, punctuation or vocabulary.

+ You will be expected to work cooperatively with other people both at work and during many assignments. Be sensitive to other people's feelings, not just your own, and always be prepared to do your fair share of the work and help other people when you can.

+ To research effectively you need to know exactly what you are trying to find and where to look. This means understanding how reference media is stored in your library as well as how to search online. Good organisation skills also help so that you store important information carefully and can find it later. And never forget to include your sources in a bibliography.

+ Making a presentation requires several skills and may be nerve-racking at first. You will reduce your problems if you prepare well, are not too ambitious and have several run-throughs beforehand. Remember to speak clearly and a little more slowly than normal and smile from time to time!

ACTION POINTS

✓ Test both your numeracy and literacy skills at http://www.move-on.org.uk/testyourskills.asp# to check your current level. You don't need to register on the site if you click to do the 'mini-test' instead. If either need improvement, get help at http://www.bbc.co.uk/keyskills/it/1.shtml.

✓ Do the following two tasks with a partner to jerk your brain into action!

- Each write down 36 simple calculations in a list, eg 8 x 6, 19 – 8, 14 + 6. Then exchange lists. See who can answer the most correctly in the shortest time.

- Each write down 30 short random words (no more than 8 letters), eg cave, table, happily. Exchange lists. You each have three minutes to try to remember as many words as possible. Then hand back the list and write down all those you can recall. See who can remember the most.

✓ Assess your own keyboarding, proof-reading, document production, written communication and IT skills. Then find out if your tutors agree with you!

✓ List ten traits in other people that drive you mad. Then, for each one, suggest what you could do to cope with the problem (or solve it) rather than make a fuss. Compare your ideas with other members of your group.

✓ Take a note of all feedback you receive from your tutors, especially in relation to working with other people, researching and giving presentations. In each case focus on their suggestions and ideas so that you continually improve your skills throughout the course.

- Don't be over-ambitious. Take account of your time-scale, resources and the skills of the team. Remember that a simple, clear presentation is often more professional than an over-elaborate or complicated one where half the visual aids don't work properly!

- If you are using PowerPoint try to avoid preparing every slide with bullet points! For variety, include some artwork and vary the designs. Remember that you should *never* just read your slides to the audience! Instead prepare notes that you can print out that will enable you to enhance and extend what the audience is reading.

- Your preparations should also include checking the venue and time; deciding what to wear and getting it ready; preparing, checking and printing any handouts; deciding what questions might be asked and how to answer these.

- Have several run-throughs beforehand and check your timings. Check, too, that you can be heard clearly. This means lifting up your head and 'speaking' to the back of the room a little more slowly and loudly than you normally do.

- On the day, arrive in plenty of time so that you aren't rushed or stressed. Remember that taking deep breaths helps to calm your nerves.

- Start by introducing yourself clearly and smile at the audience. If it helps, find a friendly face and pretend you are just talking to that person.

- Answer any questions honestly and don't exaggerate, guess or waffle. If you don't know the answer then say so!

- If you are giving the presentation in a team, help out someone else who is struggling with a question if you know the answer.

- Don't get annoyed or upset if you get any negative feedback afterwards. Instead take note so that you can concentrate on improving your own performance next time. And don't focus on one or two criticisms and ignore all the praise you received! Building on the good and minimising the bad is how everyone improves in life!

STEP SEVEN

MAXIMISE YOUR OPPORTUNITIES AND MANAGE YOUR PROBLEMS

Like most things in life, you may have a few ups and downs on your course – particularly if you are studying over quite a long time, such as one or two years. Sometimes everything will be marvellous – you are enjoying all the units, you are up-to-date with your work, you are finding the subjects interesting and having no problems with any of your research tasks. At other times you may struggle a little more. You may find one or two topics rather tedious, or there may be distractions or worries in your personal life that you have to cope with. You may struggle to concentrate on the work and do your best.

Rather than just suffering in silence or gritting your teeth if things go a bit awry it is sensible if you have an action plan to help you cope. Equally, rather than just accepting good opportunities for additional experiences or learning, it is also wise to plan how to make the best of these. This section will show you how to do this.

Making the most of your opportunities

The following are examples of opportunities to find out more about information relevant to your course or to try putting some of your skills into practice.

- **External visits** You may go out of college on visits to different places or organisations. These are not days off – there is a reason for making each trip. Prepare in advance by reading around relevant topics and make notes of useful information whilst you are there. Then write (or type) it up neatly as soon as you can and file it where you can find it again!

- **Visiting speakers** Again, people are asked to talk to your group for a purpose. You are likely to be asked to contribute towards questions that may be asked – which may be submitted in advance so that the speaker is clear on the topics you are studying. Think carefully about information that you would find helpful so that you can ask one or two relevant and useful questions. Take notes whilst the speaker is addressing your group, unless someone is recording the session. Be prepared to thank the speaker on behalf of your group if you are asked to do so.

- **Professional contacts** These will be the people you meet on work experience doing the real job that one day you hope to do. Make the most of meeting these people to find out about the vocational area of your choice.

- **Work experience** If you need to undertake practical work for any particular units of your BTEC National qualification, and if you are studying full-time, then your tutor will organise a work experience placement for you and talk to you about the evidence you need to obtain. You may also be issued with a special logbook or diary in which to record your experiences. Before you start your placement, check that you are clear about all the details, such as the time you will start and leave, the name of your supervisor, what you should wear and what you should do if you are ill during the placement and cannot attend. Read and reread the units to which your evidence will apply and make sure you understand the grading criteria and what you need to obtain. Then make a note of appropriate headings to record your information. Try to make time to write up your notes, logbook and/or diary every night, whilst your experiences are fresh in your mind.

- **In your own workplace** You may be studying your BTEC National qualification on a part-time basis and also have a full-time job in the same vocational area. Or you may be studying full-time and have a part-time job just to earn some money. In either case you should be alert to opportunities to find out more about topics that relate to your workplace, no matter how generally. For example, many BTEC courses include topics such as health and safety, teamwork, dealing with customers, IT security and communications – to name but a few. All these are topics that your employer will have had to address and finding out more about these will broaden your knowledge and help to give more depth to your assignment responses.

- **Television programmes, newspapers, Podcasts and other information sources** No matter what vocational area you are studying, the media are likely to be an invaluable source of information. You should be alert to any news bulletins that relate to your studies as well as relevant information in more topical television programmes. For example, if you are studying Art and Design then you should make a particular effort to watch the *Culture Show* as well as programmes on artists, exhibitions or other topics of interest. Business students should find inspiration by watching *Dragons Den*, *The Apprentice* and the *Money Programme* and Travel and Tourism students should watch holiday, travel and adventure programmes. If you are studying Media, Music and Performing Arts then you are spoiled for choice! Whatever your vocational choice, there will be television and radio programmes of special interest to you.

Remember that you can record television programmes to watch later if you prefer, and check out newspaper headlines online and from sites such as BBC news. The same applies to Podcasts. Of course, to know which information is relevant means that you must be familiar with the content of all the units you are studying, so it is useful to know what topics you will be learning about in the months to come, as well as the ones you are covering now. That way you can recognise useful opportunities when they arise.

Minimising problems

If you are fortunate, any problems you experience on your course will only be minor ones. For example, you may struggle to keep yourself motivated every single day and there may be times that you are having difficulty with a topic. Or you may be struggling to work with someone else in your team or to understand a particular tutor.

The media are invaluable sources of information

During induction you should have been told which tutor to talk to in this situation, and who to see if that person is absent or if you would prefer to see someone else. If you are having difficulties which are distracting you and affecting your work then it is sensible to ask to see your tutor promptly so that you can talk in confidence, rather than just trusting to luck everything will go right again. It is a rare student who is madly enthusiastic about every part of a course and all the other people on the course, so your tutor won't be surprised and will be able to give you useful guidance to help you stay on track.

If you are very unlucky, you may have a more serious personal problem to deal with. In this case it is important that you know the main sources of help in your school or college and how to access these.

- **Professional counselling** There may be a professional counselling service if you have a concern that you don't want to discuss with any teaching staff. If you book an appointment to see a counsellor then you can be certain that nothing you say will ever be mentioned to another member of staff without your permission.

- **Student complaint procedures** If you have a serious complaint to make then the first step is to talk to a tutor, but you should be aware of the formal student complaint procedures that exist if you cannot resolve the problem informally. Note that these are only used for serious issues, not for minor difficulties.

- **Student appeals procedures** If you cannot agree with a tutor about a final grade for an assignment then you need to check the grading criteria and ask the tutor to explain how the grade was awarded. If you are still unhappy then you should see your personal tutor. If you still disagree then you have the right to make a formal appeal.

- **Student disciplinary procedures** These exist so that all students who flout the rules in a school or college will be dealt with in the same way. Obviously it is wise to avoid getting into trouble at any time, but if you find yourself on the wrong side of the regulations do read the procedures carefully to see what could happen. Remember that being honest about what happened and making a swift apology is always the wisest course of action, rather than being devious or trying to blame someone else.

■ **Serious illness** Whether this affects you or a close family member, it could severely affect your attendance. The sooner you discuss the problem with your tutor the better. This is because you will be missing notes and information from the first day you do not attend. Many students under-estimate the ability of their tutors to find inventive solutions in this type of situation – from sending notes by post to updating you electronically if you are well enough to cope with the work.

PLUSPOINTS

+ Some students miss out on opportunities to learn more about relevant topics. This may be because they haven't read the unit specifications, so don't know what topics they will be learning about in future; haven't prepared in advance or don't take advantage of occasions when they can listen to an expert and perhaps ask questions. Examples of these occasions include external visits, visiting speakers, work experience, being at work and watching television.

+ Many students encounter minor difficulties, especially if their course lasts a year or two. It is important to talk to your tutor, or another appropriate person, promptly if you have a worry that is affecting your work.

+ All schools and colleges have procedures for dealing with important issues and problems such as serious complaints, major illnesses, student appeals and disciplinary matters. It is important to know what these are.

ACTION POINTS

✓ List the type of opportunities available on your course for obtaining more information and talking to experts. Then check with your tutor to make sure you haven't missed out any.

✓ Check out the content of each unit you will be studying so that you know the main topics you have still to study.

✓ Identify the type of information you can find on television, in newspapers and in Podcasts that will be relevant to your studies.

✓ Check out your school or college documents and procedures to make sure that you know who to talk to in a crisis and who you can see if the first person is absent.

✓ Find out where you can read a copy of the main procedures in your school or college that might affect you if you have a serious problem. Then do so.

AND FINALLY . . .

Don't expect this Introduction to be of much use if you skim through it quickly and then put it to one side. Instead, refer to it whenever you need to remind yourself about something related to your course.

The same applies to the rest of this Student Guide. The Activities in the next section have been written to help you to demonstrate your understanding of many of the key topics contained in the core or specialist units you are studying. Your tutor may tell you to do these at certain times; otherwise there is nothing to stop you working through them yourself!

Similarly, the Assessed Assignments in the final section have been written to show you how your assignments may be worded. You can also see the type of response that will achieve a Pass, Merit and Distinction – as well as the type of response that won't! Read these carefully and if any comment or grade puzzles you, ask your tutor to explain it.

Then keep this guide in a safe place so that you can use it whenever you need to refresh your memory. That way, you will get the very best out of your course – and yourself!

GLOSSARY

Note: all words highlighted in bold in the text are defined in the glossary.

Accreditation of Prior Learning (APL)

APL is an assessment process that enables your previous achievements and experiences to count towards your qualification providing your evidence is authentic, current, relevant and sufficient.

Apprenticeships

Schemes that enable you to work and earn money at the same time as you gain further qualifications (an **NVQ** award and a technical certificate) and improve your key skills. Apprentices learn work-based skills relevant to their job role and their chosen industry. You can find out more at www.apprenticeships.org.uk/

Assessment methods

Methods, such as **assignments**, case studies and practical tasks, used to check that your work demonstrates the learning and understanding required for your qualification.

Assessor

The tutor who marks or assesses your work.

Assignment

A complex task or mini-project set to meet specific **grading criteria**.

Awarding body

The organisation which is responsible for devising, assessing and issuing qualifications. The awarding body for all BTEC qualifications is Edexcel.

Core units

On a BTEC National course these are the compulsory or mandatory units that all students must complete to gain the qualification. Some BTEC qualifications have an over-arching title, eg Engineering, but within Engineering you can choose different routes. In this case you will study both common core units that are common to all engineering qualifications and **specialist core unit(s)** which are specific to your chosen **pathway**.

Degrees

These are higher education qualifications which are offered by universities and colleges. Foundation degrees take two years to complete; honours degrees may take three years or longer. See also **Higher National Certificates and Diplomas**.

DfES

The Department for Education and Skills: this is the government department responsible for education issues. You can find out more at www.dfes.gov.uk

Distance learning

This enables you to learn and/or study for a qualification without attending an Edexcel centre although you would normally be supported by a member of staff who works there. You communicate with your tutor and/or the centre that organises the distance learning programme by post, telephone or electronically.

Educational Maintenance Award (EMA)

This is a means-tested award which provides eligible students under 19, who are studying a full-time course at school or college, with a cash sum of money every week. See http://www.dfes.gov.uk/ financialhelp/ema/ for up-to-date details.

External verification

Formal checking by a representative of Edexcel of the way a BTEC course is delivered. This includes sampling various assessments to check content and grading.

Final major project

This is a major, individual piece of work that is designed to enable you to demonstrate you have achieved several learning outcomes for a BTEC National qualification in the creative or performing arts. Like all assessments, this is internally assessed.

Forbidden combinations

Qualifications or units that cannot be taken simultaneously because their content is too similar.

GLH

See **Guided Learning Hours** below

Grade

The rating (Pass, Merit or Distinction) given to the mark you have obtained which identifies the standard you have achieved.

Grade boundaries

The pre-set points at which the total points you have earned for different units converts to the overall grade(s) for your qualification.

Grading criteria

The standard you have to demonstrate to obtain a particular grade in the unit, in other words, what you have to prove you can do.

Grading domains

The main areas of learning which support the **learning outcomes**. On a BTEC National course these are: application of knowledge and understanding; development of practical and technical skills; personal development for occupational roles; application of generic and **key skills**. Generic skills are basic skills needed wherever you work, such as the ability to work cooperatively as a member of a team.

Grading grid

The table in each unit of your BTEC qualification specification that sets out the **grading criteria**.

Guided Learning Hours (GLH)

The approximate time taken to deliver a unit which includes the time taken for direct teaching, instruction and assessment and for you to carry out directed assignments or directed individual study. It does not include any time you spend on private study or researching an assignment. The GLH determines the size of the unit. At BTEC National level, units are either 30, 60, 90 or 120 guided learning hours. By looking at the number of GLH a unit takes, you can see the size of the unit and how long it is likely to take you to learn and understand the topics it contains.

Higher education (HE)

Post-secondary and post-further education, usually provided by universities and colleges.

Higher level skills

Skills such as evaluating or critically assessing complex information that are more difficult than lower level skills such as writing a description or making out a list. You must be able to demonstrate higher level skills to achieve a Distinction grade.

Higher National Certificates and Diplomas

Higher National Certificates and Diplomas are vocational qualifications offered at colleges around the country. Certificates are part-time and designed to be studied by people who are already in work; students can use their work experiences to build on their learning. Diplomas are full-time courses – although often students will spend a whole year on work experience part way through their Diploma. Higher Nationals are roughly equivalent to half a degree.

Indicative reading

Recommended books and journals whose content is both suitable and relevant for the unit.

Induction

A short programme of events at the start of a course designed to give you essential information and introduce you to your fellow students and tutors so that you can settle down as quickly and easily as possible.

Internal verification

The quality checks carried out by nominated tutor(s) at your school or college to ensure that all assignments are at the right level and cover appropriate learning outcomes. The checks also ensure that all **assessors** are marking work consistently and to the same standard.

Investors in People (IIP)

A national quality standard which sets a level of good practice for the training and development of people. Organisations must demonstrate their commitment to achieve the standard.

Key skills

The transferable, essential skills you need both at work and to run your own life successfully. They are: literacy, numeracy, IT, problem solving, working with others and self-management.

Learning and Skills Council (LSC)

The government body responsible for planning and funding education and training for everyone aged over 16 in England - except university students. You can find out more at www.lsc.gov.uk

Learning outcomes

The knowledge and skills you must demonstrate to show that you have effectively learned a unit.

Learning support

Additional help that is available to all students in a school or college who have learning difficulties or other special needs. These include reasonable adjustments to help to reduce the effect of a disability or difficulty that would place a student at a substantial disadvantage in an assessment situation.

Levels of study

The depth, breadth and complexity of knowledge, understanding and skills required to achieve a qualification determines its level. Level 2 is broadly equivalent to GCSE level (grades A*-C) and level 3 equates to GCE level. As you successfully achieve one level, you can then progress on to the next. BTEC qualifications are offered at Entry level, then levels 1, 2, 3, 4 and 5.

Local Education Authority (LEA)

The local government body responsible for providing education for students of compulsory school age in your area.

Mentor

A more experienced person who will guide and counsel you if you have a problem or difficulty.

Mode of delivery

The way in which a qualification is offered to students, eg part-time, full-time, as a short course or by **distance learning**.

National Occupational Standard (NOS)

These are statements of the skills, knowledge and understanding you need to develop to be competent at a particular job. These are drawn up by the **Sector Skills Councils**.

National Qualification Framework (NQF)

The framework into which all accredited qualifications in the UK are placed. Each is awarded a level based on their difficulty which ensures that all those at the same level are of the same standard. (See also **levels of study**).

National Vocational Qualification (NVQ)

Qualifications which concentrate upon the practical skills and knowledge required to do a job competently. They are usually assessed in the workplace and range from level 1 (the lowest) to level 5 (the highest).

Nested qualifications

Qualifications which have 'common' units, so that students can easily progress from one to another by adding on more units, such as the BTEC Award, BTEC Certificate and BTEC Diploma.

Pathway

All BTEC National qualifications are comprised of a small number of core units and a larger number of specialist units. These specialist units are grouped into different combinations to provide alternative pathways to achieving the qualification, linked to different career preferences.

Peer review

An occasion when you give feedback on the performance of other members in your team and they, in turn, comment on your performance.

Plagiarism

The practice of copying someone else's work and passing it off as your own. *This is strictly forbidden on all courses.*

Portfolio

A collection of work compiled by a student, usually as evidence of learning to produce for an **assessor**.

Professional body

An organisation that exists to promote or support a particular profession, such as the Law Society and the Royal Institute of British Architects.

Professional development and training

Activities that you can undertake, relevant to your job, that will increase and/or update your knowledge and skills.

Project

A comprehensive piece of work which normally involves original research and investigation either by an individual or a team. The findings and results may be presented in writing and summarised in a presentation.

Qualifications and Curriculum Authority (QCA)

The public body, sponsored by the **DfES**, responsible for maintaining and developing the national curriculum and associated assessments, tests and examinations. It also accredits and monitors qualifications in colleges and at work. You can find out more at www.qca.gov.uk

Quality assurance

In education, this is the process of continually checking that a course of study is meeting the specific requirements set down by the awarding body.

Sector Skills Councils (SSCs)

The 25 employer-led, independent organisations that are responsible for improving workforce skills in the UK by identifying skill gaps and improving learning in the workplace. Each council covers a different type of industry and develops its **National Occupational Standards**.

Semester

Many universities and colleges divide their academic year into two halves or semesters, one from September to January and one from February to July.

Seminar

A learning event between a group of students and a tutor. This may be student-led, following research into a topic which has been introduced earlier.

Specialist core units

See under **Core units**.

Study buddy

A person in your group or class who takes notes for you and keeps you informed of important developments if you are absent. You do the same in return.

Time-constrained assignment

An assessment you must complete within a fixed time limit.

Tutorial

An individual or small group meeting with your tutor at which you can discuss the work you are currently doing and other more general course issues. At an individual tutorial your progress on the course will be discussed and you can also raise any concerns or personal worries you have.

The University and Colleges Admissions Service (UCAS)

The central organisation which processes all applications for higher education courses. You pronounce this 'You-Cass'.

UCAS points

The number of points allocated by **UCAS** for the qualifications you have obtained. **HE** institutions specify how many points you need to be accepted on the courses they offer. You can find out more at www.ucas.com

Unit abstract

The summary at the start of each BTEC unit that tells you what the unit is about.

Unit content

Details about the topics covered by the unit and the knowledge and skills you need to complete it.

Unit points

The number of points you have gained when you complete a unit. These depend upon the grade you achieve (Pass, Merit or Distinction) and the size of the unit as determined by its **guided learning hours**.

Vocational qualification

A qualification which is designed to develop the specific knowledge and understanding relevant to a chosen area of work.

Work experience

Any time you spend on an employer's premises when you carry out work-based tasks as an employee but also learn about the enterprise and develop your skills and knowledge.

ACTIVITIES

The performing arts industry is one of the most competitive you will find and anyone entering the industry needs to ensure that they are highly skilled and prepared for anything. The units covered within these activities cover acting characterisation, voice technique, movement skills and the performing arts business.

Even if you are not studying some of the units within your course, you will still benefit from the activities. Dancers gain a lot from learning to develop a clearer characterisation, as do musical theatre performers. Actors can benefit hugely from a good solid understanding of the basic movement skills.

Throughout your National course you will be expected to keep log books. These will become important evidence of your progress and understanding for assessment. The first activity focuses on what should be included within log books and can be used for any of the performance skills.

When writing a logbook it is important to reflect on the rehearsal process without being too literal about it. Do not just write about the session and what you did in it. Think about how you felt with each task, what worked and what didn't and what you felt were your strengths and weaknesses.

Below is an example of how you could fill in the logbook you will be keeping throughout your course.

Your actor's log should be an analytical (not descriptive) account of your work, which you will use to reflect on and learn from your working process. It contains research information relevant to the development of your role and the performance as a whole.

Date: 16th April

REHEARSAL CONTENT

Character development: Today we used 'hot-seating' to further develop our characters. I found this exercise very helpful as it made me think about my character and I liked answering the questions as if I was that person. By having to answer questions from the class I discovered that I had not really thought about my character's family and what my relationships were like. I shall now add these facts to my character biography. I realised that I need to have a lot more information about my character.

Improvisation: Today I did an improvisation as my character with my mother in the play. We devised a scene that might have happened before the scene we are playing. I enjoyed doing this and found that it gave me a clear idea of what sort of mood I was in when our scene starts. I still need to listen more in improvisation and stop thinking about what to say next.

My strengths: managing to believe in my character more and find out some more facts to add to my research.

My weaknesses: realising that I have to listen more in improvisation and research my character in more depth.

Make sure you never just describe the activities in the lesson: your teachers know what they taught you! An assessor wants you to be reflective and know what the activities in class or in your own time meant to you and how they may have affected your approach to work.

When writing your logbook, think about the following, to ensure you are analytical and evaluate clearly:

Character development

- What vocal and physical skills are needed to play your part?
- Do you need to discuss voice?
- Do you need to discuss movement?
- Do you need to discuss your approach to your performance skills?
- Do you need to discuss the techniques you used in rehearsals (experimental techniques – Stanislavski/ Brecht inspired)?
- Do you need to discuss character/ensemble development?

Rehearsal process/self analysis/assessment

- How you did things
- Why you did things
- What worked?
- What didn't work?
- Self-assessment of your skill/skills needed to be an actor in your piece
- Strengths and weaknesses – eg of the work you did, of your group and of yourself
- How can these be improved on?

Evaluation and analysis of practical work

- Exercises you completed as part of the rehearsal process
- Character workshops
- Improvisation and rehearsal process
- Research and analysis of the play and playwrights
- Style, genre, background and contextual research

Remember to include practitioner research and your reflection on this during the rehearsal period. An example of this would be if you were studying Stanislavski. A useful way of incorporating his techniques into your logbook would be to break your rehearsal period down into sections and discuss how you approached each section reflecting on his methods. How you started looking at the 'given circumstances', for example, then focusing on the magic 'if' and so on.

UNIT 3 – THE PERFORMING ARTS BUSINESS

This section focuses on grading criteria P1, M1, D1, P2, M2, D2.

Introduction and learning outcomes

You will not be able to survive in the performing arts industry if you do not know how the business works.

Whether you have your sights set on being a professional performer or a technician, you will need to understand everyone's role within funding, administration and production. After all, even if you know how to write a professional looking CV, you will need to know whom to send it!

1 Understand employment opportunities and requirements in the performing arts sector

2 Understand different types of organisations in the performing arts sector

3 Be able to manage financial controls for a performing arts event

Content

1) Employment

Performers: eg actor, singer, dancer, director, animateur, musical director, musician

Production roles: eg producer, production manager, technical director, stage manager, set designer, lighting operator, sound engineer, wardrobe manager, scenery constructor, theatre outreach worker

Arts administration: eg producer, theatre manager, funding officer, box office staff, front-of-house, marketing officer

Training: qualifications, eg university degrees, HND (Higher National Diploma), NVQ (National Vocational Qualification), dance conservatoire, drama schools

Application procedures: eg CVs, personal statements, audition, portfolios of work, casting agencies

2) Performing arts organisations

Services: hire companies eg lighting, sound, props, scenic equipment, costume, scenic construction, script, video and music, publications, ticket booking agencies

Employment related: eg casting agencies, literary agencies, British Actors' Equity; Musician's Union, BECTU, Theatre Managers' Association

Production companies: eg The Royal National Theatre, Royal Shakespeare Company, The Royal Opera House, The Royal Ballet, Birmingham Royal Ballet, producer conglomerates, independent producers, West End theatres, large entertainment complexes, circus companies, established theatre companies, small touring companies, festival performance events, film and TV, education outreach, teaching, charity performances, community arts, pop concerts

3 Performing arts finance

Production costs: eg wages and fees, royalties, set design, lighting, sound, costume, props, rehearsal space, performance space, publicity and marketing, transport

Revenue: eg ticket prices, merchandise, programmes, catering, grants, sponsorship, workshops, special events

Funding: private sector, eg individual producers, producer associates (conglomerates), private investors, franchises, branded products, advertising, celebrities, patronage, ticket prices; public sector eg national arts councils, regional arts councils, lottery grants, local authority, sponsorship, patronage

Grading criteria

P1 describe a range of employment opportunities and functions in the performing arts

This means that you will need to give an account of the characteristics and qualities [describe] of different job roles within the performing arts industry [range of employment opportunities], indicating for each role what they do and why [function].

M1 explain in detail a range of employment opportunities and functions in the performing arts

To achieve a Merit you will need to make clear in detail some revealing and relevant facts about the roles [explain].

D1 critically comment on a varied range of roles, responsibilities and functions in the performing arts

To achieve a Distinction, your accounts will need to examine thoroughly the job roles and make judgements on the positives and negatives of the employment [critically comment]. You will also need to make sure you include different types of roles from performers, to production, to arts administration [varied range], ensuring that you explain who and what they are accountable for [responsibilities].

P2 identify the training requirements and experience for a career path and produce application material

This means you need to discover and establish [identify] the training and professional experience needed to successfully fulfil a chosen job role within the performing arts industry. You also need to complete suitable application material such as a CV.

M2 research the most appropriate training requirements and experience for a career pathway and prepare suitable application material

To achieve a Merit, your investigation into the training requirements for a role will need to show a discovery of facts and reach conclusions [research] on a suitable or proper way [appropriate] to get a job. Your application material will need to be fit for purpose [suitable].

D2 research a comprehensive range of training requirements and experience based on extensive research and prepare application material to a professional standard

To achieve a Distinction, your investigation into a job role will demonstrate a complete understanding [comprehensive] of the different opportunities for training and professional experience, which is detailed and far-reaching [extensive]. Your application material is written and/or presented as if you were actually applying for a professional job.

ACTIVITY 1

The performing arts industry can seem complicated, as no two arts organisations, production companies or theatres necessarily have the same employment structure and lines of management.

The following activities are to help you understand the different job roles and develop awareness of how they might change within different environments and sizes of businesses.

Task 1

Listed below are 20 job titles from the theatre industry. Draw up a table like the one below and sort them into the three categories by writing them under the heading that best describes their primary function.

Actor, production manager, stage manager, finance director, sound engineer, dancer, box office manager, lighting operator, front-of-house assistant, wardrobe manager, singer, technical director, producer, musician, front-of-house manager, marketing officer, scenery constructor, theatre manager, animator, theatre outreach worker.

Performers	Production team	Arts Administration

Task 2

Now answer these questions:

1 Were there any roles you didn't understand, ie you didn't know what they did?
2 Were there any roles that you felt could have gone in more than one category? Why would this be?
3 Which category of roles was the easiest for you to identify? Why?

Do some research to fill in any gaps in your understanding of the roles; there are also many more you can add to this list. Don't worry if some roles still don't easily fit one category. A producer could easily be written into both production and arts administration categories.

ACTIVITY 2

If you want to have a long-lasting career as a performer, you have to be talented and adaptable and prepared to continually assess your skills and recognise areas of self-development.

Task 1

What skills do performers need to work in the performing arts industry? Draw up a table like the one below to help you assess professionals' essential and optional skills.

To be a ...	Essential	Optional
Stage or film actor		
Singer		
Dancer		
Musical theatre performer		
Holiday entertainer		

Task 2

Now study your favourite TV or film performer, someone you aspire to be like. Do as much research as possible into their past history, making notes on what age they started, what training they had, productions they have been in and so on.

Make a list of skills they have needed to develop to a professional level to survive and get to where they are now.

Task 3

Collate your findings for Tasks 1 and 2 to present to your class. You could put these tables into PowerPoint slides or draw them up on a whiteboard and/or flipchart.

The sharing of this research with your colleagues is really valuable, because the more you know about performers who are successfully working in the industry, the better a picture you will have of what you will need to do for your career.

Task 4

Think about what your ideal work would be as a performer and make a list of what skills are essential and optional. Use a table like this to write an action plan for which areas you will need further training and focus!

My personal skills audit

ESSENTIAL	
Skills required	**Action**
eg Singing	Start singing lessons
OPTIONAL	
Skills required	**Action**
eg Be able to ride a horse	Take a couple of lessons while on holiday

From this activity you should come to realise that good singing, dancing and acting skills are really important to all performers. Professional dancers (even those who have trained with a contemporary dance company) will find themselves at some point on stage having to sing along in a chorus. There are very few professional actors that haven't had to sing at some point in their career – take Dame Judy Dench and Al Pacino, for example. Both are known for their amazing acting skills but both have also starred in musicals at some point in their career.

ACTIVITY 3

Not everyone has to be a performer and in the spotlight to have a fulfilled and successful career in the performing arts.

There are considerably more jobs behind the scenes and for this activity we will concentrate on the arts administration roles of a theatre.

Task 1

On the next page there is a diagram of the organisational structure of a theatre, with some job titles missing. Where there is a missing job title there is a brief description of the role to help you identify the title from the list below.

Work out where the following job titles fit on the diagram:

- finance director
- board of directors
- marketing officer
- front-of-house manager
- sales and marketing director
- chief executive
- box office manager
- theatre manager

Task 2

Every arts organisation, production company and theatre is different. For example, in most theatres there is no artistic director and the theatre manager or chief executive takes a more creative role in programming. In some theatres the theatre manager would be in charge of the box office.

You will find hundreds of websites for companies on the internet, all with information on who works for them and what their job title is.

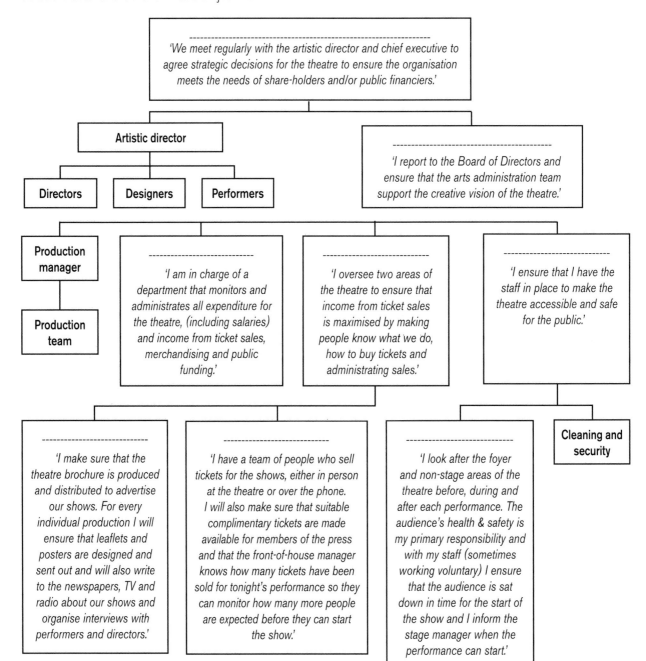

1 In groups of four decide on two theatres and two independent touring theatre companies to research.

2 Each group member should then research one organisation, making notes on the number of people working for the company (full-time/part-time/freelance) and their job titles.

3 Present your findings to the group.

4 Group discussion – consider the main differences in who they employ and why.

ACTIVITY 4

The diagram below shows the creative team involved in creating a new production of *Star Wars: the Musical*. In charge of the whole process would be the producer, with the director leading the creative team in making decisions for the 'look' of the show.

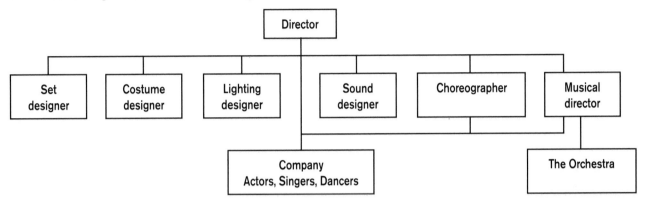

Task 1

The table on the next page shows a time line from the start of pre-production and opening night. All the members of the creative team should have finished their main roles in creating the production by the time a public audience sees it for the first time.

Read the following quotes from members of the creative team and, using your own version of the time line on the next page, put a cross in the box to show when that person has had to be involved during the production process, and a single diagonal line if their attendance wasn't crucial.

Choreographer

'I attended the first meeting with the rest of the production and creative team and helped with the casting. But my work didn't really start until the first rehearsal. The director wanted me around throughout the rehearsal process. Thankfully I didn't have to attend any other meetings, the director just told me what he wanted. The dance captain took over from me once opening night was over.'

Musical director

'I attended a meeting where I met the rest of the creative team and played a big part in the casting sessions. I had to be at every rehearsal to support the director. The band call is when I get to have fun and once we are in the theatre I am conducting the orchestra. I am still working on the show.'

The company

'We attended casting and were notified when rehearsals started. The first rehearsal was great to meet everyone. Technical rehearsals were really slow but I am enjoying still working on the show.'

Costume designer

'I work very closely with the set designer, having to attend all the same meetings and rehearsals.'

Lighting designer

'I attended all the production and design meetings as I like to know how changes will affect my lighting. The great thing with this job is once the rehearsals start I really can't do anything until I see a final run-through in the rehearsal rooms. I helped focus LX during the technical fit-up and was present for all the tech rehearsals making major changes throughout. We were still making changes up until an hour before first performance.'

The orchestra

'Not only do the musicians get paid more but we don't have to worry about castings or the long rehearsal period. I simply got a call from a fixer asking me to attend the band call, we didn't even have to attend all the boring technical rehearsals. Still working on the show.'

Set designer

'Most of my work has to be completed before the first rehearsal. From the first production meeting I worked closely with the costume designer to bring together the design concept, attending regular design meetings with the director and finally presenting the model box to the creative team and producers. Apart from the odd visit to see how construction is going, I attended the technical fit-up and rehearsals and was keen to see the show open and the audience reactions.'

Sound designer

'Apart from some pre-production planning to do after the first production meeting, I am the least involved until I join the lighting designer to watch a run-through in the rehearsal rooms. I sent a colleague who will end up engineering the show to the band call and I supervised the technical fit-up and rehearsals. It was important for me to attend the first night to ensure that the sound engineer was operating successfully with a full audience in the theatre.'

	Choosing creative team	Production briefings	Design meetings	Presentation of model box	Casting	Production meeting	First rehearsal read-through	Rehearsals (six weeks)	Progress meetings	Run-through in rehearsals room	Band call	Technical fit-up	Technical and dress rehearsals	First performance	Subsequent performances
Director	X	X	X	X	X	X	X	X	X	X		X	X	X	X
Choreographer															
Musical director															
Set designer															
Costume designer															
Lighting designer															
Sound designer															
The company															
The orchestra															

ACTIVITY 5

The production team is one of the busiest and most exciting parts of any theatre. Without these people we would not have lighting, sound, a set or even a safe stage!

Production managers have a demanding job as they receive information from the director and designers and transfer this information to the relevant production department.

Task 1

As Production Manager you have just attended a production meeting with the Creative Team. You have made notes in the meeting on technical requirements and changes that affect your eight departments. Copy the information below and draw a line from each action to the correct head of department.

Production meeting – 14th May 06

A1, S1 – One of the actors has to light a real match, he does not smoke.

A1, S2 – There are now two more spear carriers at the back of the stage – total 12.

A1, S3 – The castle wall is too short and needs to be raised by 1250mm.

A1, S3 – Because of the raised castle wall, LX Designer has requested for wide angle parcans on LX3.

A1, S4 – The knights' helmets need to be changed again, they still can't see enough. This will also affect the placement of radio mics!

A1, S5 – The most complicated scene for flying has had to be changed and the back wall does not need to be flown within this scene (this may mean we can loose a flyman each night).

A2, S1 – The colour for the banquet hall is not correct, it needs to be a much darker purple. LX may need to be re-coloured to compensate.

A2, S2 – There is not enough time for Peter to get around to Stage Left for the voice of the dragon. Can the microphone be moved to SR?

The designer has requested for two smoke machines to be used, one each side of the stage.

Stage Manager
Deputy Stage Manager •
Assistant SMs

Technical manager
Stage crew • Flymen

Construction manager
Deputy • Carpenters • Metal workers

Head scenic artist
Deputy • Assistant scenic artists

Head of props
Deputy • Prop makers

Chief LX
Deputy • Assistants/Operators

Head of sound
Deputy • Assistants/Engineers

Wardrobe supervisor
Cutters • Assistants • Dressers • Maintenance

ACTIVITY 6

The landscape of performing arts education or training for school leavers has changed considerably since the days when you would either go to university to study a degree or drama/dance school to study professional skills and get a school diploma. There is so much choice now for young people that it can seem very confusing.

The usual courses provided are:

Certificate of Higher Education
The first year of a degree course.

National Diploma
Not to be confused with the BTEC National Diploma you are on! This is a professional qualification validated by Trinity College and usually offered at some dance schools in musical theatre or dance.

Higher National Diploma
BTEC continued: a two-year vocational course, which, if completed with high grades, can lead to the third year of a degree (often called a top-up).

Foundation Degree

Very similar to a Higher National Diploma, with an emphasis on work-related learning. A two-year course for vocational students that has to have a clear pathway for successful students to move onto the third year of a degree course.

Degree

A three- or four-year course, where graduates obtain a bachelor's degree usually in Music or the Arts (BMus or BA).

Postgraduate

Courses for graduates which can be one/two years extra after a degree where you gain a master's degree.

It is never too early to start thinking about your future. The UCAS website is an excellent resource.

Universities & Colleges Admissions Service

www.ucas.com

Task 1

Visit the UCAS website and search for courses in performing arts. Make a list of six institutions for each of the above qualifications.

For some drama and dance schools you don't apply through UCAS and have to apply direct. Widen your search for courses by visiting the following websites:

National Council for Drama Training

www.ncdt.co.uk

The Conference of Drama Schools

www.drama.ac.uk

Council for Dance Education and Training

www.cdet.org.uk

Try to work out what the differences between qualifications really are – how your qualification will be delivered and assessed, how much it will cost and so on.

Task 2

Choose three of the courses that you have found and to your class or group of peers feed back why they interest you.

Consider the following information for each course:

- the institution and location
- the qualification you would receive at the end of the course
- course content
- style of delivery (academic, vocational…)
- lecturers
- open days
- would they interview you?
- facilities
- student numbers (course and department)
- progression (what are their students doing now?)

ACTIVITY 7

On the opposite page are four advertisements for musical theatre performers which use different methods open to the industry.

Task 1

Read each advertisement and note where it was published. From reading the advertisements, make a judgement on the quality of the work offered from what has been said.

SHAKESPEARE FOR CHILDREN

THEATRE COMPANY

Annual Auditions
Male/Female – Actors/Singers/Dancers
for
UK & International Tour
August – July
Please send /Photo to
****

Advertised: SBS & PCR

Buddy Holly Tribute Show

needs
Musical Theatre Performers
for UK and Ireland tours July – December

Good strong voices important, ability to play an instrument
and dance/move well an advantage

Contact ****************************

Advertised: The Stage

OPEN CALL

Male/Female
Musical Theatre Performers

for Stephen Sondheim's classic

Into the Woods

UK Number 1 Tour

Auditions:

Wednesday 14 June at 9 am
The Prince of Wales Theatre

Bring CV and Photo

DO NOT SEND CVs INTO THE OFFICE!

Advertised: The Stage & SBS

********* Theatre Company is looking for two
musical theatre performers (male and female) for their
forthcoming production

UK tour September – December
Equity Minimum

Please send CVs and Photos to ******************

NO EMAILS PLEASE!

Advertised: SBS, PCS & CastNet

49

1 What makes you want to apply?
2 What makes you think twice?
3 What is easy about the audition?
4 What is hard about applying?

You can take into account the method of advertising the work.

Task 2

You are in the basement café in the Actors Centre, London. You have bumped into
four other musical theatre performers who have just entered the industry. During the
conversation you find out the following information about each one.

Dan
Got an OK agent from his drama school showcase but hasn't got many castings so
joined CastNet. Regularly reads *The Stage*.

Jess
Joined CastNet too as she didn't get an agent and so has to find all her own castings.
She pays to receive PCR every week and has been to lots of castings but nothing that
big or well-paid yet.

Jonathan
A relatively new agency signed him up six months after he left drama school. His
parents are loaded and so he has a subscription to PCR, *The Stage* and is on two
different web-based casting services. He regularly sends out CVs and photos to
production companies. Always working, but small productions.

Harriet

A large agency signed her up at the start of her last year at drama school. They have introduced her to several large casting agencies, and she has had lots of castings for adverts and TV, but no work yet. She is broke from having to buy new photos for the agency. She reads *The Stage* when her flat-mate buys it.

All four of these performers need the work advertised in these four castings. Try to answer these questions:

1 Which of these people would get to know about each casting?

2 Would this rely on someone else to think they were suitable or interested (an agent or casting director)?

3 Which person would have the best chance of finding out about all the castings?

SBS

Industry-standard information on castings sent out to all casting directors and agents. It is not available to actors directly. The information within SBS tends to be more reliable than other publications. Production companies are not charged to advertise their casting information.

The Stage

A weekly newspaper for the entertainment industry which is available from some specialist newsagents or by subscription. It has a jobs section where some production companies will pay for an advertisement to announce castings. www.thestage.co.uk

PCR – Production and Casting Report

A weekly newsletter (now with email updates) that actors can subscribe to. It is free for production companies to advertise their castings but not to companies advertising products and services.

CastNet

CastNet is an example of a web-based database of actors who have registered and paid for their CV to be online. Production companies can either log onto the site and browse through the actors online or announce a casting and CastNet will then email or send hard copies to the production company of suitable candidates. It is a free service for the production companies to use. Good web-based casting directories are choosy though. Not everyone can pay to be included – only those who have been to an accredited drama school and/or had paid professional work are considered.

ACTIVITY 8

Everyone needs a CV! When you start out in the industry you will need a good photo and a clear and concise CV to hand out and send to potential employers, whether you are a performer or work behind the scenes.

Task 1

Create your own CV. Make sure it is produced on a computer and you include the following:

- **name**
  contact details – address, telephone numbers, email
- **photo**
- **vital statistics** – DOB, playing range, weight, height, hair colour, eye colour, build, ethinic origin, nationality
- **training credits**
- **additional skills**

Further information

Photo – one of the biggest expenses for a young actor is getting a good photo taken and having it professionally duplicated at the size of 10 inches tall by 8 inches wide. For your CV, don't go to any expense, simply get hold of a digital camera and put a small head shot at the top left hand corner of the page.

Credits – this is the list of shows you have been in and should include – the year, whether it is film/theatre/radio/advert, title, role, director, production company. As you are not a professional yet, most, if not all, of your credits will be while in training or amateur. You should always make sure this is very clear – NEVER pretend something you have done is professional!

Additional skills – you never know when being a good strong swimmer, or being good at accents will come in handy. But don't lie – plenty of actors have been caught out and have never ridden a horse, wasting expensive production time.

Task 2

In class or a group collect together everyone's CVs.

You are now a producer working for a small theatre company, currently in production and casting for a show.

Read through two of the CVs.

1 Is there one that you immediately prefer?

2 Why?

Make a list of positives and negatives of each CV. Take into account both the content and layout.

3 If you had 300 CVs to go through for one job, would any of these go straight into the bin?

There are no right or wrong answers. Your observations on what gives a good impression and what doesn't are what's important.

Honest and constructive feedback to each other can be tough to take but it is far better to know now what makes a good and bad CV than risk yours being filed in the round filing cabinet under the production assistant's desk!

ACTIVITY 9

Using the table to help you, research arts organisations, theatres and production companies to find at least two examples of each type.

Presenting/Receiving Theatres	Producing Theatres	Independent Production or Theatre Companies
Theatres that would not typically produce their own shows, but instead they negotiate to receive productions from other producing theatres or independent production/theatre companies. It would not be unusual though for them to produce their own panto, for which they would hire extra production staff and creative team in for the production period.	Initiate their own productions, have permanent staff within the production team. May tour their productions to other Receiving Theatres. May consider co-producing a production with an outside company, but rarely happy to present other shows without involvement. Producing theatres can also be called Repertory Theatres, Repertoir Houses or Stagione.	Initiate their own productions, who then rent theatres to receive their shows. Most companies would only have a small core of permanent staff office based, hiring rehearsal rooms and extra production staff when in production. Other names sometimes used are Touring Theatre Company or Theatre in Education Company (TIE).
1	1	1
2	2	2
3	3	3

ACTIVITY 10

There are three main unions to support you depending on what type of employment you have in the performing arts industry:

www.bectu.co.uk
www.equity.org.uk
www.musiciansunion.org.uk

Choose one union and complete the following table:

Name of union	
Web address	
Who is it for?	
How much is it to join?	
What age can you join?	
What conditions do you have to meet before they will let you join?	
Is there a student option?	
List any benefits from being a member in order of importance to you	

ACTIVITY 11

You are a theatre manager of a medium-sized regional receiving theatre in the UK. You need to increase income to help pay the bills and have decided to produce this year's panto in house.

Because visiting companies usually bring all their own equipment, the theatre will need to hire in more equipment and specialist technical help.

The panto is *Peter Pan* and will run from December 1st to February 1st.

Task 1

Write a list of all the servicing companies you will need to work with.

You have decided to hire everything to create the show so the list needs to be fully complete.

Task 2

Where possible you have decided to use only local companies, in the hope that you will be able to negotiate a good discount.

Write a list of selling points to drop into your conversation showing why they should give you a good deal. What could you offer them that wouldn't cost you anything?

Task 3

For this particular panto there is one very specialist service provider that would be very unlikely to offer any kind of discount.

What do the company do?

Why do you think they are unlikely to offer a discount at this time of year?

What employment-related services would you also need to contact?

ACTIVITY 12

Below are two extracts from the current *Union Rates for Commercial Theatre Tours* as published by the TMA and the relevant unions for actors and musicians in this country.

TMA/Equity Commercial Theatre

Actor (Rehearsal)	£300
Actor (Performance once nightly)	£315
Actor (Performance twice nightly)	£340
Subsistence	£90
Weekly Touring Allowance	£169

Understudy obligation (per role/week)	£13.03
Understudy performance (per perf.)	£19.53
Swing Dancer (per week)	£16.31
Dance Captain (per week)	£29.31

(From September 4, 2006 – provided by Stage One)

TMA/Musicians' Union

Musician (Performance once nightly)	£355.55
Musician (Performance twice nightly)	£371.71
Subsistence	£114.00
Weekly Touring Allowance	£169.00
Porterage – 1 Instrument	£10.34
Porterage – 2 Instruments	£20.57

(From April 15, 2006 – provided by Stage One)

As a professional it would be really important that you could check whether you are being paid correctly.

Task 1

Listed below are four scenarios describing how much you have worked for different shows. Calculate your total wages for each job.

Scenario 1 – small touring play (actor)

You were employed for four weeks in central London for the rehearsal period and then a six-week UK tour. The show was short and suitable for schools and therefore played twice nightly.

Scenario 2 – musical (musician)

You were asked to take over from another musician half way through a 20-week UK tour. You played flute and clarinet, one performance a night.

Scenario 3 – musical (dancer)

You were asked to replace a dancer half way through a 20-week UK tour. You had one week of rehearsals in London prior to joining the tour performing once nightly. Because of further illness in the cast you were made dance captain for the last four weeks of the run.

Scenario 4 – large-scale play (actor)

You were asked to play a small part in a large-scale touring play, however you had the responsibility of understudying two of the main leads. Rehearsals lasted six weeks in Plymouth, before a 30-week tour, once nightly. During the tour you had to understudy for the main roles in 36 performances.

ACTIVITY 13

Good publicity and marketing of shows is crucial to their success. It doesn't matter how good your actors are, how amazing your set or how catchy the songs; if people don't know about the show, they won't come. Even if you get some leaflets printed, if the design is wrong, you may not attract the right kind of audience to see your show and they will leave disappointed.

ANSWERS to Activity 12 Task 1

Scenario 1
£4,794

Scenario 2
£6,591

Scenario 3
£6,164

Scenario 4
£22,059

Task 1

Collect as many brochures, leaflets, fliers or posters advertising performing arts productions as you can. If you do not have a theatre that is local to you, try collecting marketing materials from art galleries, cinemas and so on.

In a group of no more than four, spread all the brochures and leaflets out on tables and analyse them considering the following questions:

1 What do you like about them?

2 What don't you like?

3 What size is the leaflet?

4 Is the leaflet printed on both sides?

5 What is the quality of paper like?

6 Does the leaflet have all the dates on for the entire tour?

7 Does the leaflet make you want to go to see the show?

8 How does it target the correct audience?

Try to be really critical of the leaflets. You may find it helpful to do this task in a group, sharing resources that you have collected and discussing your reactions to them. Sharing feelings about something in a group can counteract individual taste.

Task 2

The table on the next page shows the costs of printing leaflets and fliers with an internet-based printing company. The prices are very competitive but they expect artwork to be emailed over to them print-ready, which means that these prices do not include any design costs.

Study the pricing for different sized leaflets. The following information will help you understand the data.

A6	DL	A5
Postcard size – four per A4 page. This size of leaflet is usually only used by clubs and pubs for advertising to young people. Some theatre companies opt for this if they are wanting to target this age group. It's also cheaper to print.	Tall and thin – three per A4 page. This is the usual size used for leaflets in London's West End. The display stands have to be much smaller due to space in venues. Big expensive productions will have large leaflets folded down to DL.	Half an A4. This is the size traditionally used by regional theatres. Display stands are not as cramped and as more shows are coming to each theatre, leaflets can have more information on them to help sell each show.

Leaflets can be printed on just one side or both sides. 130 gsm and 350 gsm refers to the weight or thickness of the paper the leaflet is printed on. As a guide, normal paper used in a printer is 80 or 90 gsm, so 130 gsm is thick paper and 350 gsm is card.

Scenario

Your production company has to produce leaflets for a variety of productions in the year (touring, West End, week runs, single nights and so on). The leaflets have to be produced at minimum cost but without compromising the design and look that could affect people's opinion on the quality of your shows.

Discuss in your group the different strategies you could take with different types of shows, using the leaflets you have collected to help.

These are just a few examples of the hundreds of questions that should be going through your mind:

1 If the show is really commercial does it need lots of space to sell it?

2 Does the thickness and quality of paper affect the perception of quality for different shows?

3 Could the extra postage costs for heavier leaflets affect your decision?

4 Long-running West End shows can have large print runs; however, what changes would mean you have would have to do a re-print?

QTY	A6			DL			A5		
	1 side	2 sides		1 side	2 sides		1 side	2 sides	
	130GSM	130GSM	130GSM	130GSM	130GSM	130GSM	130GSM	130GSM	130GSM
250			£50			£90			£100
500	£40	£55	£60	£50	£85	£100	£60	£100	£115
1000	£50	£65	£80	£65	£100	£125	£75	£125	£150
5000	£60	£75	£100	£80	£115	£150	£100	£150	£200
10,000	£100	£130	£150	£150	£200	£225	£175	£275	£300
15,000	£140	£195	£225	£225	£300	£325	£265	£335	£450
20,000	£175	£260	£300	£300	£370	£450	£340	£395	£600
50,000	£385	£455		£472	£500		£580	£619	
75,000	£485	£550		£575	£635		£720	£765	

5 If you are touring regional theatres they will each want between between 5,000 and 20,000 leaflets for each show. What could you do to bring these down to one larger but cheaper print run?

ACTIVITY 14

When producing an accurate budget to finance a show from either private or public money, a producer will divide the costs into two areas.

First, the capital or production costs. These cover everything that will cost the production company money up until the show opens. Capital costs sometimes include previews and opening/press night as well, as these performances do not generate normal income. Secondly, the producer will work out the weekly running costs.

Create a table like the one on the next page and sort the following costs according to whether they are capital or running. It is important that you question why. Some may need to go in both!

List of costs to be sorted:

Salaries – performers
Salaries – technical staff
Salaries/fees – director
Salaries/fees – designers
Salaries – musical director
Salaries – choreographer
Royalties – writers, director, designers

Set construction
Set hire
Prop purchasing
Prop hire
Lighting purchasing
Lighting hire
Sound purchasing
Sound hire
Rehearsal space
Theatre hire
Publicity and marketing
Transport

Producers must raise at least the full predicted capital costs and six-weeks' running costs before going into production. Most production companies that get into financial trouble are those that have gone into production before the money is in place and rely on ticket sales, which are so unpredictable!

Capital costs		Weekly running costs	
Cost	Why capital?	Cost	Why running?

ACTIVITY 15

You have just been employed by a theatre company as a production manager.

On your first day you attend a production meeting where the creative team discuss the possibility of touring one of their previous shows again for next season. You are asked to produce a spreadsheet of the weekly running costs for this production, and you quickly make notes from the creative team on what should be included within the weekly costs.

Sort the notes (below) from your meeting and create a spreadsheet outlining all the costs mentioned, producing a weekly total. You may think of other items that are not mentioned that you wish to include. Use the costing form from previous activities and the internet to help.

The production is the classic play Miss Julie (seven performances a week)

Salaries

3 x cast – 1 male 2 female (equity minimum + £60 each per week) 2 x understudies (1 male 1 female) will be actor ASMs (equity min. Don't forget understudy obligation fees). Company stage manager – does not have to be budgeted for (works full-time for the company).

Set

Needs to be transported in 7.5 tonne truck that CSM can drive. We also need to hire a backcloth that cost 3 years ago £150 a week, and 10 stage braces and weights – est. £6 each.

Lighting & Sound

Need to budget to take some extra lanterns with us (est. £200). All the theatres have the sound equipment we need.

Props

Each performance a cooked dinner needs to be made and est. 10 plates and 5 cups get smashed. One of the chairs used to always get broken and only last two weeks (est. replacement £60).

Royalties

£60 per night for script, est. £30 for music.

Contingency

For costume repair, gaffer tape, colour gel for lighting, smoke fluid, paint for set touch ups

Printing

15,000 A5 leaflets (double sided) needs also to be included per week

Description	est. cost
LX - lantern hire	£200.00
Etc.	

ACTIVITY 16

Balancing how much you can spend on a production and how much you think you will make on ticket sales is a difficult balancing act.

In previous activities you have been working out the costs for different elements of a show. However, if your predicted ticket sales do not cover all these costs, then you will have to start cutting budgets for salaries, set building, costumes and so on.

Task 1

Ticket prices are usually fixed by market forces. Amateur productions have the greatest flexibility here to undercut professional productions. This is because they don't have to pay one of the largest bills – salaries!

Using the internet, research ticket prices in the West End and regional theatres for different kinds of shows, making sure you are only looking at professional productions.

Try to get lots of examples so that you can see if there are any patterns in pricing between different types of shows, eg family tickets for pantos.

Are there any clear differences between ticket pricing in the West End and regional theatres (eg you usually have to pay full price for children in the West End)?

Task 2

Once a producer has a clear idea of what kind of prices can be charged for tickets, the company will estimate an income at each theatre based on ticket sales for previous shows of the same type. It would be very foolish of a producer to take a play to a theatre estimating that he will sell 80% of the seats at full price, if the theatre had warned that they never sell more than 40% for a play and that most tickets go to OAPs who receive a discount.

In pairs work out the estimated income for each performance of the following shows. The calculation for the first one has been shown to help you.

Musical revue evening

Information from Box Office Manager:
'usual ticket prices are £15 and £10 concessions, last time a similar event sold 80% of tickets. The theatre has 400 seats.'

Average ticket price (£15 + £10 ÷ 2 =)	£12.50
Maximum potential income (£12.50 × 400 seats =)	£5,000.00
@ 80% Predicted Sales (£5,000.00 ÷ 100 × 80 =) or (£5,000.00 × 0.80 =)	£4,000.00

Now your turn:

Large-scale musical

Information from Box Office Manager:
'usual ticket prices are £27 and £18 concessions, last time a similar event sold 75% of tickets. The theatre has 1500 seats.'

Average ticket price	
Maximum potential income	
@ % Predicted Sales	

Play

Information from Box Office Manager:
'usual ticket prices are £20 and £16.50 concessions, last time a similar event sold 50% of tickets. The theatre has 600 seats.'

57

Average ticket price	
Maximum potential income	
@ % Predicted Sales	

Ballet

Information from Box Office Manager:
'usual ticket prices are £40 and £30 concessions, last time a similar event sold 40% of tickets. The theatre has 2000 seats.'

Average ticket price	
Maximum potential income	
@ % Predicted Sales	

Task 3

What other sources of revenue does your local theatre produce (for example, interval drinks)?

ACTIVITY 17

Theatres and production companies must find some way to fund their latest production. It would be very rare for any company or individual to have all the money themselves to fund a project.

Task 1

Read the following quotes from people who regularly help to finance performing arts productions. Decide whether the quote describes public or private funding and then write the funding title (the words in **bold**) in the table provided.

'I work for the **NATIONAL ARTS COUNCIL** and I regularly receive detailed funding applications for touring productions. I have strict criteria to assess the applications as I am spending tax payers' money.'

'I am known as a **PRIVATE INVESTOR** or "Theatre Angel". I have had a successful career in starting small business, but my passion is live theatre. I regularly invest small amounts into new West End shows. On many of these I have lost all my money but one particular show has been open now for 14 years. I invest because I have a disposable income and I love attending opening nights!'

'I represent a large airline that regularly provides **SPONSORSHIP** to touring productions or large arts organisations. We see a benefit to our company in being associated with the arts at a very high standard and a place that has international recognition. We currently sponsor the Royal Opera House in London.'

'I represent a **REGIONAL ARTS COUNCIL** that receives applications from companies that wish to produce shows within my region. We are especially keen to hear from producers who are creating something new and exciting, and which will encourage new audiences.'

'I am an **INDIVIDUAL PRODUCER** who has made a lot of money over my career in production. I currently have two long-running shows in the West End, and have just finished working on a very successful play that toured the UK. I have a two million pound fund that I keep to re-invest into new productions, I am always careful to ensure that if my next production loses money my other shows are not at risk.'

'I work in an office selling **ADVERTISING** space for theatre programmes. For many theatres, both regional and West End, we supply a valuable steady income stream.'

'I help assess applications for **LOTTERY GRANTS** in the UK. It is a very long process as the process is very strict in what we can and can't fund. At the end of the day, we are a charity that raises money from selling lottery tickets to the public and we have to make sure we don't waste this valuable resource.'

'**TICKET PRICES** are set by the producer and theatre manager on booking the show. I know that the producers have very high costs, but it is sometimes quite difficult for my box office staff when they have someone complaining about the ticket prices for some shows.'

'The **LOCAL AUTHORITY** has limited funding to support the arts, therefore we are especially keen to hear from projects that meet particular local needs. In the past we have funded a small *theatre in education* tour around schools with a performance on bullying and we regularly support a local theatre festival that encourages some tourism.'

Public	Private

Task 2

The funding of the arts with public (tax payers') money is a very controversial subject. In a group, discuss the use of public funding in this country for the arts. Use the following statements to help stimulate debate:

1 'Why did all of that public money get wasted on the Royal Opera House when the majority of the ticket prices are still far too expensive for any normal tax payer to afford?'

2 'It's important that public money preserves the arts for future generations. A piece of visual art like an oil painting can go into storage for decades and will still be the same when it is eventually presented in an exhibition many years later. Performance art has to be handed down from generation to generation. We close the Royal Opera House and we lose opera for ever!'

3 'I went to see the ballet the other day at my local theatre because the radio station announced half-price tickets. It was ridiculous, the tickets still cost me £30 each and the theatre was empty! It was an amazing spectacle to see so many people on stage and in the orchestra, but why should public money keep shows like this touring when people don't want to go and see them?'

4 'There is nothing wrong with commercial theatre and the creation of art having to be profitable. Both Mozart and Shakespeare created works of art that in their day were simply produced to make people laugh or cry. If I can't get arts council funding for my commercial shows to entertain my audiences, why should some contemporary drama production receive it that no one understands anyway?'

ACTIVITY 18

This final activity brings together all that you have learned in previous activities.

Choose a production that you have been in at school/college either recently or currently. The production can be anything: play, musical, music evening, variety performance etc.

We are going to pretend that you have been asked to recreate the show professionally, and have to prepare a budget clearly outlining the costs and the potential income.

This activity can be completed as a group project, working in pairs or on your own.

Task 1

Make a list of everything that was used for production, including props, costume, set and so on.

Make an estimated guess as to how much it would cost to buy or hire these items for a professional production.

Task 2

We will assume that no one got paid to be in your school/college production. However, we need to cost out how much it would be to employ you and your fellow students professionally. Use the actor salaries outlined in Activity 12 to help you with this. You will also need to decide how many weeks of rehearsals, working six days a week, your professional cast would need.

Don't forget to pay your director, musical director and other team members. For this activity estimate an amount; however, to get a Distinction you will need to do some serious research, when you come to your final assignment.

Task 3

Don't forget any extra costs, such as rehearsal rooms, theatre hire and staffing to run your school/college theatre for performances.

Task 4

Now try to work out your income from ticket sales and then subtract the total costs from Tasks 1 – 3 from this amount.

At this point it is likely you have a balance sheet that shows a huge deficit (shortfall).

Task 5

Think about what changes you could make to try and break even (break even means where income and costs cancel each other out – therefore no shortfall).

Here are a few questions to help:

1 Could you reduce the cast size?
2 Could any of the technical costs be reduced?
3 Could you apply for any public funding?
4 Could you encourage any private finance?
5 If you did more performances, would this help?
6 If you performed in a larger theatre, would this help?
7 If you spent money on marketing the show, would this help?
8 Would your production ever be able to break even?

Budgets are produced to help theatres and production companies to answer these very questions. For a budget to be successful it requires detailed and comprehensive research and a creative approach to trying to make the balance sheet turn into profit.

UNIT 17 – DEVELOPING VOICE FOR THE ACTOR

This section focuses on grading criteria P2, M2 and D2.

Introduction and learning outcome

As an actor your voice is one of you most important tools, it's a delicate instrument that without you looking after it could cut short your career. A good voice technique will be the foundations to a successful career as an actor. Unless you have the skills to use your voice correctly to deliver different expression in a controlled way, you will not have the technique to portray your character.

You will find the ability to record yourself and listen back invaluable to properly assess your abilities in practical work and recognise areas of personal development. Sound recordings can be done really easily now with the use of mobile phones, or a dedicated dictaphone or even small video, all relatively inexpensive these days.

2 Know how to devise a regular programme of physical and vocal exercises.

Content

Breathing and relaxation: posture; body awareness; breath control; breath capacity; facial relaxation; body relaxation; specialist techniques, eg Alexander technique, yoga

Technique: tone; pace; pitch; pause; projection; inflection; modulation; intonation; articulation; resonation

Grading criteria

P2 devise and conduct a programme of vocal and physical exercises with support and guidance

This means you will have invented, planned and carried out [devise and conduct] a programme of vocal and physical exercises, helped by your teacher/tutor throughout.

M2 devise and conduct a programme of vocal and physical exercises with minimum support and guidance

To achieve a Merit, you will have needed very little help from your teacher/tutor.

D2 autonomously devise and conduct a programme of vocal and physical exercises

Distinction students will have invented, planned and carried out a programme of vocal and physical exercises entirely on their own, with no help from their teacher/tutor [autonomously].

ACTIVITY 1

PERSONAL VOCAL ASSESSMENT

Choose a small passage about two or three paragraphs long from a book, magazine or newspaper, and record yourself reading it out loud.

Task 1

Copy the chart below and complete it to make an assessment of your voice from the recording.

I think I have ...	strongly disagree			strongly agree		What vocal faults are evident?
1 Good, clear voice production	1	2	3	4	5	eg speaking too quietly
2 Good articulation	1	2	3	4	5	eg mumbling words and sloppy articulation
3 Good pace	1	2	3	4	5	eg spoke too slowly or too quickl
4 Good variety in tone and pitch	1	2	3	4	5	eg speaking in a monotone
5 Good breath control	1	2	3	4	5	eg out of breath

Ask yourself whether you feel that these vocal faults meant that your performance had no real atmosphere and/or demonstrated a lack of understanding of the text.

Task 2

Now try Task 1 again in a large room, placing your recording device at the opposite end to where you perform. The larger the room the better, especially if the space has acoustic issues that you need to overcome – for example, a church or school hall has reverberation. Good actors can ensure that their vocal technique still allows an audience member at the back of a large theatre to hear them and understand every word.

Task 3

Make a list of any improvements you need to make and research relevant exercises for this in the books suggested for this unit.

Task 4

Why not revisit this activity at the end of each term? You might surprise yourself on how you have improved!

> ### LINKS
>
> Include evidence of this activity in your logbook (if you are not studying this unit, then it is still valuable for any acting log books).

ACTIVITY 2

ANALYSING TWO VOICES

Task 1

Use a case study of someone you know, friend or family, and listen to them speaking. Why do you like their voice? Why do you not like it?

See if you can write a list of words that come to mind when you hear their voice.

Make a table like the one opposite to help focus on what makes the voice interesting or annoying.

Task 2

Now try the same thing with your favourite character in a movie.

Task 3

Any professional writer or actor never stops working, they find every opportunity to observe others and identify vocal characterisations that they might later use in a production. Observe groups of people at parties, in the classroom, at work and anywhere else you happen to be. What vocal characteristics dominate the room and how do they affect your opinion of the people they belong to?

ACTIVITY 3

STRETCHING YOUR VOICE

Try to do this activity for 30 minutes every day.

Task 1

- Breathe in through the nose and then out on a prolonged 'hah'.
- Breathe in through the nose and then out on a prolonged 'ah'.

Repeat the above, using your middle register, increase the volume and keep the sound going for as long as you can.

	Observations	
	Task 1 – friend or family	Task 2 – famous person
What kind of tone is the voice?		
How fast or slow do they speak?		
Do they pause a lot?		
Do they find it difficult to project?		
Do they articulate their words?		
What is the pitch like?		
Do they emphasise certain words?		
Do they speak on one tone?		
Do they have any specific difficulties when pronouncing certain words?		
Do you like their voice? If so, why? Write down at least three reasons.		
Do you dislike their voice? If so, why? Write down at least three reasons.		
Is the voice loud/voluminous?		
Is the voice quiet?		
Is the voice deep?		
Is it high/low?		
Is it strong?		
Is it weak?		
Is it shaky?		
Is it husky?		
Is it crisp?		
Is it clipped?		
Is it drowning?		
Is it nasal?		
Is it squeaky?		
Is it crackly?		
Is it raspy?		
Is it distorted?		

- Breathe in through the nose and then out using 'hah' but going up the scale and then down the scale.
- Breathe in through the nose and then out using 'mah' going up and down the scale.

Repeat the above and when you feel comfortable increase the volume, remembering not to lose the tone of your voice.

Task 2

Go through the alphabet from B using the vowels:

eg   bah, bay, bee, bi, bo, bu
          cah, cay, cee, ci, co, cu
          dah, day, dee, di, do, du

It would be a good idea to write all of the letters out as above and then try to speak them faster and faster – making sure you are articulating each sound.

Task 3

Practise the following tongue-twisters in order to give your speech precision.
    Red leather, yellow leather,
    Red lorry, yellow lorry.

For fluency with words that are formed by the lips, practise saying:

    Peggy Babcock

Practise speaking out loud the passage below, which combines a number of difficulties. The more you do it, the more fluent you will become.

    I am the very pattern of a modern Major-General;
    I've information vegetable, animal, and mineral;
    I know the Kings of England, and I quote the fights historical,
    From Marathon to Waterloo, in order categorical;

    I'm very well acquainted too with matters mathematical,
    I understand equations, both the simple and quadratical,
    About binomial theorem I'm teeming with a lot o' news,
    And many cheerful facts about the square of the hypotenuse.

    I'm very good at integral and differential calculus,
    I know the scientific names of beings animalculous.
    In short, in matters vegetable, animal, and mineral,
    I am the very model of a modern Major-General.

(Gilbert & Sullivan)

ACTIVITY 4

See how many more tongue-twisters you can find and practise them. Start with some simple ones and then see if you can impress your classmates with some difficult ones. Remember to always think about the following:

1 What is happening to my mouth when I say this tongue-twister?

2 Where is it forcing me to place the sound?

3 Why is it difficult to say it quickly?

At the end of the week, using a similar chart to the one below, write up your development as if you were a doctor writing a prescription. Think about the diagnosis – for example, not being able to sustain or control breath for more then six counts – and decide on the cure.

Problem	Cure
Tongue-twisters - cannot complete the following: Red leather, yellow leather, blue leather.	Take 5 mins each day to practise this twister. Sit quietly and break it down. Think about each word and where it is placed in your mouth. Keep saying it slowly and focus on it until you can build it to a faster rhythm.

By the end of the week, you will have been able to find out what you need to work on as an actor and will be able to devise your own individual warm-up plan that suits you.

LINK

Your logbook must demonstrate that you have developed your own regular programme for physical and vocal exercise.

ACTIVITY 5

The following text will be useful for the tasks below:

Henry V (CHORUS)

Now entertain conjecture of a time
When creeping murmur and the poring dark
Fills the wide vessel of the universe.
From camp to camp, through the foul womb of night,
The hum of either army stilly sounds,
That the fixed sentinels almost receive
The secret whispers of each other's watch.
Fire answers fire, and through their paly flames
Each battle sees the other's umber'd face.
Steed threatens steed, in high and boastful neighs,
Piercing the night's dull ear; and from the tents
The armourers, accomplishing the knights,
With busy hammers closing rivets up,
Give dreadful note of preparation:
The country cocks do crow, the clocks do toll,
And the third hour of the drowsy morning name.

Task 1

Group work – all get in a circle and speak through the passage, going clockwise one at a time, changing person at each punctuation mark. Some will have more to say than others.

Things to notice from this are:

- the length of a 'thought'
- the rhythm that single words give
- the quality of the words

Do the same exercise as above but now sing the passage round. Notice how the sound and meaning of the words back each other up.

Task 2

Solo work – use the same passage and speak it through, raising your arms on the first and last word in each line. This will make you aware of the fullness of the words, which in turn contribute to the thoughts in the passage.

ACTIVITY 6

You can only perform successfully on stage or in front of a camera if you are physically and vocally relaxed. Try the following tasks on your own to help you to learn to relax. You may also find the exercises helpful to prepare for performance.

Task 1

Physical

Before going to sleep at night:

Practise relaxing your whole body. Lie flat on your back with arms by your sides and eyes shut.

Start with your toes – wiggle them and then relax.

Repeat this, going up through ankles, legs, hips, tummy, shoulders and finally neck.

At the end of this you should feel sleepy and relaxed.

On getting up in the morning:

From a standing position, gradually stretch your arms right up above you and then relax.

Repeat this three times.

Let your head drop onto your chest then relax forward from the waist, so that your hands are dangling on or near the floor.

Keep your legs relaxed.

Slowly raise yourself up, uncurving the spine vertebra by vertebra – your head should be the last to come up.

Breathe in and exhale deeply on the sound of 'ah'.

Task 2

Vocal

Push your lips out and then stretch them back in a wide smile so that you feel your cheekbones are raised and your teeth show. Repeat three times.

Massage your face all over with your hands.

Imagine you are chewing a large piece of bubble gum and really move your mouth round as you do this.

Imagine that you have pieces of chocolate caught in your teeth and try to get them out with your tongue.

Stick your tongue out. Raise it to your nose, drop it to your chin and then move it from side to side.

Finally do a huge yawn and make the sound of a yawn.

ACTIVITY 7

Task 1

When you read a speech for the first time, it can be hard to work out what is happening. This results in a very monotone delivery, which in everyday life we don't use.

Using a speech that you are working on in class or a poem:

- Record the extract for the first time without focusing too much on light and shade.
- Now record it again and make sure you change the tone on each line.

Listen to both recordings and determine which it the most interesting to listen to.

Task 2

Now record a normal conversation between two people and analyse how many times they change the tone. See if you can list what happens to their voices when they are excited, happy, sad, annoyed, fed up and so on.

ACTIVITY 8

Task 1

Once of the most important things when reading and learning a script is punctuation. Punctuation will tell you how the line should sound; if used incorrectly it will change the playwright's intention for the line and could result in a poor performance.

Choose a poem to use for this activity and read it out loud without any punctuation. Now try it again, but this time standing in front of a chair:

- Jump up into the air – every time you get to a full stop.
- Sit down in the chair – every time you get to a comma.

It doesn't matter if you jump from a standing or seated position, the exercise is to force you to pause before continuing through the poem. This will help you to focus on the punctuation in the poem and see how it affects the delivery when used correctly and incorrectly. Now take a monologue that you are working on and do the same.

Task 2

Using the same poem:

- Speak in a relaxed voice whilst doing as many physical activities as you can – eg lifting someone, lying down and trying to get up, without using your hands, crawling under tables – trying to keep your voice fluent and smooth.
- Now let positions affect the voice. Use the rhythm of physical activity to affect the voice – don't be too precious about making it sound beautiful.

Get one of your family members to describe what happens to your voice when you:

- resist letting the activity affect your voice
- let the activity affect your voice

Record this in your logbook. Now do the same with people in your class. You should start to see a pattern of what happens to the voice when you try to resist the act of physical activity.

ACTIVITY 9
CORRECTING COMMON VOCAL FAULTS

Task 1

Nasal tone

Nasal tone is caused by a lack of flexibility of the soft palate, which is at the back of the roof of the mouth.

- Breathe in through the nose but with the mouth open and then breathe out through the mouth.

Notice how the soft palate and the tongue come together when you breathe in, and then separate quickly when you breath out. Repeat this six times.

Open the mouth to make the sound 'ah' and then add 'ng' to it – so you will be saying 'ahng'

Notice that that soft palate has to come down to form the 'ng' and then be released to form the 'ah'. Repeat this six times.

Now reverse the sound so that you are saying 'ngah'. Repeat six times.

Task 2

Lisp

A lisp is sometimes caused by not having sufficient control over the tip of the tongue so that it wanders out when it should be kept inside the mouth. Try the following:

- Press the tip of the tongue against the lower teeth, mouth open, and try to push the teeth out, not moving the tongue-tip at all.
- Then touch each side of the mouth at the back with the tip of your tongue, now at the centre and then push it right out as before.
- Repeat six times.
- With the teeth together, make a hissing sound, keeping the tongue inside and making sure that the teeth do not part.

Make up as many words with the 'S' sound as you can – eg steps, wasps, wisdom, seize and so on. Repeat each word six times.

ACTIVITY 10

VOCAL EXPRESSION – MAKING THE VOICE INTERESTING!

Task 1

Work with a partner for this. First decide who is number 1 and who is number 2. Try to read the script below. There are no words, just sounds.

You are trying to turn these sounds into a real conversation between two people. You both need to decide beforehand what you are talking about. Take notice of the punctuation as this will help you. Pronounce the letters as they are written so that the first line sounds like 'Bee see dee!'

No. 1   B C D!
No. 2   B C D?
No. 1   B C D!
No. 2   O…
No. 1   A B C D E F G?

No. 2   H I.
No. 1   H I?
No. 2   H I J K.
No. 1   L M N O P! Q R S? T U?
No. 2   X Y Z.

Task 2

Swap partners and this time you can ignore the punctuation marks and make your own decisions on how to say each line, using the following scenarios:

- One of you is frightened and the other thinks the whole situation is very funny.
- Both of you are madly searching for something you have lost.

Practise this until you can do it without the sheet and then add gestures and movements to your scene. Notice the changes in the tone and inflection that you use in your delivery in order to get your meaning across.

ACTIVITY 11

For this activity you will need to do some vocal observation to use in a group activity on character development.

Task 1

Research

When listening to different types of voices you should be taking note of the following:

Pace Do they speak at speed, or slowly and deliberately?	for example: a newscaster might speak slowly and a children's presenter might speak in a fast and excited way
Tone Is there a 'warm' quality to the voice or is it quite 'cold' sounding?	for example: commercials on television are a good source for this
Accent Do they have any specific accent you could imitate?	for example: cockney, northern and so on – a character from EastEnders would have a cockney accent

You should choose the following voices to listen to and then try to sound like them:

- a radio presenter
- a character from Coronation Street or EastEnders
- a character from Neighbours (note Australian accent)
- a television presenter

Task 2

In your groups, each take it in turn to introduce one of your characters – do not say your name but describe your job and see if the rest of the group can guess who you are.

Use the above exercise when you are considering a character you are developing for either a scripted or devised piece of drama – take into account what vocal qualities you think your character might have.

ACTIVITY 12

Imagine that you are a speech therapist and you have to give an analysis of different people's speeches and a diagnosis of any problems.

Watch any of the 24-hour news programmes on television and study several people who are being interviewed. Don't choose to study the interviewer, these people will have had voice and speech coaching! Choose someone who is not usually in the media spotlight. If you have digital TV you can sometimes watch the highlight stories on a loop, which can give you more time to study their faults.

Things to look out for:

TONE	Do they change the tone often? Are they more monotone?
PACE	Do they read quickly? Are they able to still use punctuation correctly if they are speaking fast?
PITCH	Is their voice high? Low?
ARTICULATION	Do they pronounce their words?
INTONATION	Do they stress certain words?
DICTION	Are you able to understand them? If they were on the radio, would you be able to hear every word they said?
ACCENT	Does this affect the way they say certain words? Do they have difficulties with any words?
PROJECTION	Ask them to stand far away from you or you could try it outside. Can you still hear them? Does their voice sound strained?

At this point in your studies you need to be focusing in on the reasons for the vocal problems and what exercises and techniques can improve them.

It is often easier to hear difficulties other people have than your own. Once you have diagnosed a variety of people, ask your fellow learners to do the same for you.

ACTIVITY 13

In order to expand your vocal capacity you need to be aware of resonating your voice.

Group work

- All stand round in a circle and start humming – take a good deep breath before you start and be careful not to raise your shoulders.

If you are placing your voice nicely forward you should feel your lips tickling.

- When you have established a good humming tone, everyone in the group should keep the humming going and slowly walk backwards, making the circle larger and larger. Once you have walked as far as you can go, you should all slowly start walking in again till you reach your original place in the circle and then stop humming.

The object is to keep the tone and volume steady while you are moving.

- When back in the circle, take another deep breath, hum as before, and beat your chest with the flat of your hand to encourage the 'sound'. Repeat this using 'mm' and 'ah' sounds.

Develop the above by experimenting with Tarzan cries while beating the chest with alternative fists – Tarzan style!

ACTIVITY 14

PROJECTION EXERCISE FOR TWO PEOPLE

Try and find a variety of spaces and see how the voice differs in each space:

- an empty corridor
- outside in a car park
- in a cupboard
- in a toilet
- in a busy shopping centre
- in a bar/nightclub
- in a canteen
- in a restaurant
- on an empty stage
- in a busy theatre

Choose a poem, go to each place and take it in turns to recite your poem, asking the other person to stand away from you and listen. See what happens to your voice and breathing in each of the different spaces. Do you need to strain more? What happens to your voice if you don't support your breath?

Don't strain but do push the voice, making the shapes with your mouth as wide as possible to help your partner work out what you are saying.

ACTIVITY 15

BREATHING AND VOCAL WARM-UP FOR GROUP WORK

Task 1

The whole group should stand in a circle – everyone is to:

- do a huge silent yawn
- then yawn and allow a small sound to come out
- then yawn very noisily

Next the whole group should:

- do a small sigh
- then do a longer sigh
- and finally exaggerate the sigh and make a loud noise

Task 2

Divide into pairs – one of you sighs while the other one yawns. Focus on your partner and the sound you are making.

Task 3

Divide the group into two halves.

- One group is to decide on a specific noise such as groaning, fearful, dragon-like etc. When they have decided, this group will breathe in – yawn – and then do their chosen sound.
- The other half of the group have to guess what sort of noise it is meant to be.
- Repeat this with the other half of the group deciding on a specific noise.

ACTIVITY 16

GROUP WORK IN VOCAL TECHNIQUES WITH YOUR SCRIPT

Task 1

The whole group should stand in a large circle and choose one person to start.

- The first person should choose a line from the scripted work.
- They should then choose a person standing opposite in the circle – saying their name and then saying the line, imagining that they are 'throwing' their line over to them.
- This person should then choose another person opposite them in the circle and do the same with one of their lines.

Notice what happens to your tone and inflection as you do this – also you should concentrate on projecting your voice without straining.

Task 2

If you have a scene with another person try practising your lines by sitting back to back to each other and 'whispering' your words. Again take notice of what happens to your tone and inflection. This is good way of making sure you are really listening to your partner.

Task 3

During the last days of rehearsals when you are all familiar with your scripts it is a good idea to use one rehearsal session just for lines. All sit around in a circle and in a relaxed manner, as if you were just having a conversation, and go through the play. This is a good way to really use the words without moves, props and gestures getting in the way. It is also a good exercise for making sure you are really listening to each other and reacting to what is said to you.

ACTIVITY 17

Use the following voice and speech quiz as revision for yourself or as part of a group activity.

1   What is the name given to the cavities which help to amplify the voice and give it tone?

_____

2   Name them:

a   _____

b   _____

c   _____

d   _____

3   The diaphragm is... (choose one)

■ Muscle   ■ Ligament

■ Cartilage   ■ Membrane

4   Which voluntary muscle in the mouth plays a major role in articulation?

_____

5   What does 'articulation' mean?

_____

6   On exhalation the ribs move...   _____ and _____

7   On inhalation the ribs move...   _____ and _____

8   On inhalation the diaphragm...   _____ and _____

9   On exhalation the diaphragm...   _____ and _____

10   What is another name for the voice box?

_____

11   The height and depth of vocal sound is called?

_____

12   What is known as the 'life force' and vital to sound production?

_____

13   What is the name given to the muscles attached to the ribs?

_____

14   What is another name for the windpipe?

_____

15   What is the name given to other group of consonants?

_____

16   What does 'modulation' mean?

_____

17   How can you create atmosphere and tension in a text?

_____

18   What part/s of the vocal system are employed in producing a simple 'S' sound?

_____

ACTIVITY 18

Task 1

In a group of friends or family, sit in a circle and ask each person to tell a story. It can be a happy story, a sad story, a scary story etc.

- Carefully listen to each person's story.
- Using a spider diagram, determine the genre of the story and annotate the diagram explaining what happens to the voice during the telling of the story

For example:

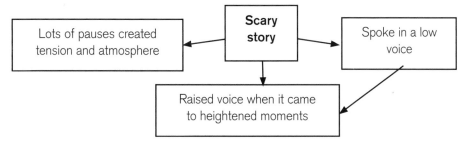

Task 2

Discovering the power of the voice

In groups decide on an environment such as the jungle or the beach and focus on all the sounds you might hear in those places. Recreate all of those noises without using speech. Only use sound. Decide on which sounds will be louder than others. See if you can come up with an amalgamation of sounds that would be obvious to a listener if they could not see you.

A story may develop but it is quality of sound that makes it interesting. Look at the light/shade of the performance. See what happens to the voices when communication happens and when moments that need to be stressed happen.

ACTIVITY 19

PERSONAL WARM-UP PLAN

See if you can complete the following task every day for a week. At the end of each day, list any improvements. At the end of the week, use your warm-up plan and lead your class with it. See if you can notice any difficulties they have. Try and pinpoint what they need to work on.

Task 1

Start by de-tensing your whole body. Take each body part separately and see if you can tense it and then release it. Every time you do this, breathe in and then exhale when you de-tense. Once you have done the whole of your body, lie there and think about the following questions:

ANSWERS to Activity 17

1 Resonators 2 Chest, Throat, Head Nose 3 Muscle
4 Tongue 5 Express Clearly 6 In and down 7 Out and up
8 Contract and flattens 9 Relaxes and arcs 10 Larynx
11 Pitch 12 Breath 13 Intercostals 14 Trachea
15 Continuants 16 Variety 17 Using pause, differing pitches
and range 18 Tongue, Teeth, Lips, Breath, Diaphragm
– EVERYTHING!

1 Do I feel relaxed?

2 Where do I hold the most tension in my body?

3 Have I released any tension I was holding in my body?

4 Am I able to connect with each body part individually?

Now you need to focus on breathing. Start by focusing on where you need to breathe from. Think about what happens when you breathe in and out. Spend about 5 minutes on this. Then start to breathe in for a number of counts. Breathe in for 4, hold for 4 and then out for 4. Think about how it feels at each point. See if you can improve your counts and control your breath.

Once you have completed your counts, ask yourself the following questions:

1 Was I able to sustain my breath for all of the counts?

2 Was I able to improve my counts throughout the week?

3 Were there any points where I struggled to breathe from my diaphragm?

Now add sounds to your breathing counts. Breathe in for 4, hold for 4 and then breathe out for 8 making an 'ah' sound. Then do the same and try an 'err' sound and then finally an 'oo'. Each time you make the sound, think about what happens to your mouth and where the sound is placed.

Now you need to focus on your face, mouth, teeth, tongue and lips. Think about all of these areas and try and focus on them individually using a variety of exercises. Try using the following:

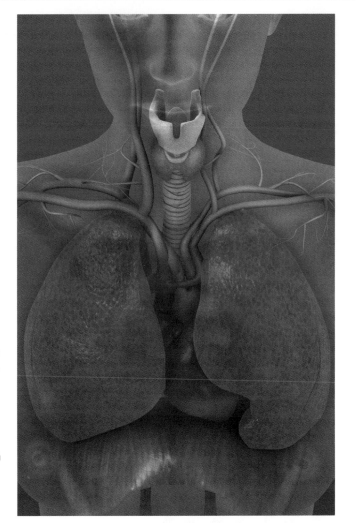

PA	–	lips
TI	–	teeth
KA	–	front roof of mouth
BA	–	in front of teeth
DE	–	bottom of mouth
GA	–	back of the throat

Think about what happens to your mouth when you say all of these words. Try and distinguish where the sound is focused in your mouth. See if you can find some more exercises that help.

Task 2

Now it's up to you to devise your own personal plan. Remember to include all the exercises you would have completed during the lessons and from the study guide. When devising your warm-up plan think about the following:

■ I need to make sure I have released all the tension in my body, therefore have I included exercises that ensure that I am free from all tension?

■ Have I thought about my face? Mouth? Teeth? Tongue? Lips?

■ Have I incorporated breathing exercises into my warm-up plan that allow me to improve my breathing counts?

■ Have I found a difference in my projection when my voice is supported by breath? If so, how will I incorporate exercises in my personal warm-up plan that will enable me to sustain this?

■ Have I found a range of tongue-twisters that I can practise on a daily basis?

■ Have I made sure that when practising my tongue-twisters I have tried to do as many as I can do with one breath?

■ Have I included any pitch, pace and rhythm exercises as part of my personal warm-up plan?

- Have I included my humming exercises?
- Have I managed to improve in any of my vocal exercises from the study guide and if so have I listed them in my reflective logbook?

When writing your own plan, try to list as many exercises and techniques to start with and then work through them and see which ones work best for you. Think about what areas you feel you need to work on.

You will have had some experience diagnosing problems that other people have with their voice. Now think about your own. Using recordings of dialogue that you used for previous activities, listen to them again and self-diagnose your own areas for development. For example, if you have a problem with projection, make sure you include more projection exercises as part of your individual warm-up plan. If you have difficulties pronouncing 's' as you have a lisp, make sure you include vocal exercises that will help you to overcome it.

This unit focuses on grading criteria P1, M1 and D1, P2, M2 and D2.

Introduction and learning outcome

The activities in this section are here to help you with developing your characterisation. Whether you are actually studying Unit 20 or any other Acting unit, or even Musical Theatre and Dance, you will find these activities invaluable for improving your understanding of the craft of acting.

1 Know how to develop characterisation as an actor

Content

Research and development: analysis of text to build character/role; improvisation; observation; research material to build information about character; units and objectives; analysis to build character's through-line; communication with director and/or company to develop interpretation of the role

Skills and techniques: application and experimentation with movement; voice; gesture; emotional range and investment; interaction and responsiveness; adoption and application of appropriate acting style; use of space, use of time, use of weight, dynamics; inner and outer characteristics; consideration of function of characterisation

Grading criteria

P1 research a character, drawing simple conclusions about the nature of the role

This means you will need to investigate your role to discover information and reach conclusions about the character [research], making observations of the qualities that make the person.

M1 research a character, accounting for the creative process in developing a role

To achieve a Merit, you will need to also keep a record [accounting] of the series of steps [process] in developing your characterisation of the role – for example, a logbook.

D1 research a character, giving a comprehensive and reasoned account of the creative process and fully supporting their conclusions about the role

Distinction students will ensure their logbook of the creative process will be wide ranging and complete [comprehensive], demonstrating during the creative process why decisions were made in the interpretation of the role [fully supporting their conclusions].

P2 develop rudimentary skills and techniques for the realisation of a character/role, demonstrating some grasp of the specific demands upon the actor of particular texts, in relation to the style of acting

This means you will have developed basic skills and techniques to create a suitable characterisation (qualities that make somebody interesting in terms of personality, behaviour, appearance…). Your decisions in creating the character will show that you have reacted to different plays and styles of performance and that it is appropriate. For example, your physical movements will be different if you are playing a wealthy gentlemen in Pride and Prejudice than if you were playing a teenager in Hollyoaks.

M2 develop sound skills and techniques for the realisation of a character/role, demonstrating a sound grasp of the specific demands upon the actor of particular texts, in relation to the style of acting

To achieve a Merit, students will have developed a good level [sound] of skills and techniques to create and make real [realise] their role in a play/scene/monologue. Students will show a good understanding of what makes the role real and what they need to do to perform it successfully, ensuring that it is appropriate to the style and/or period of the play.

D2 develop advanced skills and techniques for the realisation of a character/role, demonstrating a comprehensive grasp of the specific demands upon the actor of particular texts, in relation to the style of acting

Distinction students will have developed a high level and comprehensive set of skills and techniques to make real their role within a play/scene/monologue. They will have a wide understanding of different styles of acting and texts and how these should be used to help create an appropriate character.

ACTIVITY 1

FOR USE WITH SCRIPTED SCENES

Task 1

Using your script, take time to answer the following questions:

- **Who** am I? (the name of your character)
- **Where** am I? (where is the scene set)
- **What** do I want? (what my character wants to happen in this scene)
- **Why** do I want it? (why my character wants the above to happen, what difference it will make to him/her)
- **How** am I going to get it? (what this means is what your character is going to use in order to get what he/she wants – for example, by bullying, by praising etc.)

The above are the five basic questions that Stanislavski would ask his actors about the character they were playing. This would encourage them to think deeply about their roles and 'find the truth' needed for naturalistic style.

Task 2

The magic 'if'

Write a brief description of the situation your character finds themselves in. Then write a description of how you would behave if you were in the same situation – thinking about how you move, speak, feel and so on.

Example:

My character's situation: My name is Sandra and I am in a café waiting for my mum. After a big row I have refused to go home and have been staying with a friend but have agreed to meet her.

How I would behave: I would be feeling very worried because of not knowing how my mum is going to react – I would, therefore, sit at a table in the corner trying to hide a bit from other people in the café.
I think my nerves might make me feel a bit cold, so I would be huddled up.

ACTIVITY 2

It is important that you understand your character's life before you attempt to make choices about how you are going to play them. Your script is the best place to start as it gives you clues about the character and how they live. Once you have found all of these clues, you then need to make further choices on what they like and dislike, their aspirations, feelings towards other people etc. Try to make connections: if the character reminds you of someone famous or even someone in your life, use that person and base your decisions on them. If it is someone completely alien to you and you really don't understand 'who they are' or 'where they are coming from', then that's when research can be really handy.

As an example, suppose your character was a British soldier who had just come home from Iraq and had been exposed to a lot of harrowing things and was dealing with shell shock. Where would you begin? If you knew nothing about the profession or the experiences they might have had, you would need to do as much research as possible, so that your individual character choices would be truthful.

Using the script and further research, start building your character's life in a scrapbook.

Get a big blank book and start to build a scrapbook. Imagine that someone was going to build a scrapbook about you, think about all of the things you have seen, done, enjoyed or disliked and transfer all of that on to your character. Remember, everything should be truthful. Do not decide that your character is from Birmingham, if the script says that they have an American accent.

Start by thinking about and adding the following to your scrapbook:

- how the world looks through their eyes and start to build their life
- where they were born
- pictures of where they grew up
- what they wanted to be when they were growing up
- their family tree – this could be a little diagram of who was related to whom in the script. If it is never decided, then use your imagination
- pictures of people that really mean something to them
- pictures of idols
- favourite songs
- favourite colours
- favourite paintings, films, plays, books
- people that have inspired them
- passions/interests, hobbies
- things/pictures that mean a lot to them
- favourite foods
- friends
- memories – difficult ones, happy ones (this could be done using words, pictures, letters)
- favourite clothes
- poems, words that inspire them, make them happy, sad etc.
- pictures, letters from first loves
- favourite holiday destinations – places that make them feel happy or sad (places that stir an emotion in them)

Include in your scrapbook characters you spend a lot of time with – make decisions about their favourite things and remember to include how you feel about them

Do not be afraid to make individual choices. Once you believe that this character really exists, you will be able to make relevant acting choices in the rehearsal room.

ACTIVITY 3

Read the script, and then read it again making notes on all the connections between characters, including ones we never see you meet. You need to make decisions on how you feel about all of these characters. Remember, a good playwright will always make decisions on characters that will assist your understanding if you know the text inside out.

Task 1

Draw up a chart. You could use the template below or find your own way of recording the details.

Character name	Who they are	What do they want from me?	What do I want from them?	How do I feel about them?	Do I get what I want from them by the end of the play?

Task 2

Try drawing a spider diagram, where you put your character in the middle and draw arrows out connecting you to everyone in the play.

Remember to comment on your relationship with each character by finding the clues to how you feel about them in the text.

ACTIVITY 4

To discover the purpose of every speech by your character, you need to look for clues in the script. Some scripts will have more information than others: if the information is not in the script, then you should use your imagination to fill in the blanks.

Task 1

The given circumstances

Using your script, try to answer the following questions:

1 What do other characters in the script say about you?
2 Do any stage directions describe your home, habits, possessions or appearance?

Useful quote from Stanislavski: 'Remember, for all time, that when you begin to study each role you should first gather all the materials that have any bearing on it, and supplement them with more and more imagination, until you have achieved such a similarity to life that it is easy to believe in what you are doing.'

ACTIVITY 5

The easiest way to make interesting actor choices is to start observing human behaviour. Not only does it teach you to really open your eyes and see what characters are living around you, it also allows you to understand how complex one character can be and how many different emotions and feelings they could experience in just ten minutes, let alone in a two-hour play.

Task 1

Go to a café or any public place such as your local or school library, school canteen, gym etc and take a small notepad and pen. Find somewhere to sit where you can quietly observe people's behaviour without being obvious about it. Use the questions below as a guide to help you observe interesting details about people. See if you can come up with any observations of your own.

- What is your character's gender?
- What are they wearing?
- How does this affect the way they move?
- How do they sit? Stand?
- How do they move? Quickly? With importance?
- What facial expressions do they use?
- What do these facial expressions tell you about how they are feeling?
- How do they deal with people around them?
- How do they behave in different situations?
- How different are they when they are with someone they know as opposed to a stranger?
- How comfortable are they with their physicality? Are they confident with their body shape?
- Do they have any specific gestures that they keep repeating?
- When communicating with other people, are they able to look them in the eye?
- Do they have a loud or quiet voice?
- Do they speak over other people or do they prefer to listen?
- How do they react if confronted?
- How do they deal with difficult situations?

- How do they deal with different people who are higher or lower status than themselves?
- What happens to their physicality and voice when they are with someone they like?
- What happens to their physicality and voice when they are with someone they dislike?
- How does their voice affect their behaviour? Is it quiet or loud? Is it brash? Is it demanding?

You may not be able to answer all of the questions if the person you are observing is on their own. Try and observe lots of different people and see what clues someone's mannerisms can give you about how they are really feeling.

Task 2

Using the same questions, apply this technique to someone on TV. Look at reality programmes such as *Wife Swap* and *Big Brother* and focus on physicality and behaviour. See how these people respond to everyone around them. What happens to their physicality and behaviour when they are with someone they like/dislike?

Even if you don't find anyone you think is like your character, just get into the habit of seeing someone else's life. You will only be able to see a small snippet of their life in your observations, so use your notes and create a more 3D picture of their life.

Task 3

Use clues to fill in further detail not available from simple observation. For example, if a woman is sitting alone, has no wedding ring on and seems fairly young, do not decide that she is 64 with 16 grandchildren! Make believable choices.

- What family do they have?
- What do they do for a living? Are they a student?
- Do they have any identifiable habits?
- What are their wants?
- What are their needs?
- What are their ambitions?
- What makes them happy? Sad?

ACTIVITY 6

You are a detective and you have been given one hour to find as many clues about your character as possible.

- Using your script, write down everything that you say about yourself that exposes your character.
- Now write down everything other people say about your character.
- Now write down what you say about other people.

Once you have got all these clues, get together with the rest of your group and feed back to each other about what you have found. You could even do it in your detective character.

Remember, a good playwright will always use a set-up and pay-off process. This is where they will suggest something in a scene and then answer further on in the play.

They will also do the same with character traits. How one character behaves in one scene may trigger the development of another character in another scene.

ACTIVITY 7

Find a bag/briefcase that you think your character might use regardless of gender and start to fill it. Put everything in it that you think your character might have in their bag. For example:

- train tickets
- petrol receipts
- food receipts
- toiletries
- make-up
- personal music players
- hair bands
- chewing gum
- food
- medicine

Try to put in as many clues as possible.

Once you have produced your bag, give it to another member of the cast and ask them to see what they can determine from the bag. What clues can they find about the character whose bag it is? Ask them to be as detailed as possible.

For example, if the character has make-up in their bag:

- Where is it kept?
- Is it in a little bag?
- Is the bag well kept?
- Is the make-up new?
- Is it an expensive brand?
- Is it clean?

Remember, everything in the bag should determine what kind of person your character is.

ACTIVITY 8

Once you have gathered all the information about your character, you can begin to transform yourself physically into the character. You can use this process for all characters, including non-speaking parts.

Task 1

Think of an animal that has some qualities in common with your character. Questions to ask yourself are:

- What is the animal's tempo – is it slow moving or quick moving?
- What is the animal's primary sense – sight, smell or hearing – and how does it show this?
- What shape does the animal make (draw a physical shape made by this animal)?
- How does it move or act?
- How does it eat?

Choose one word to describe the animal's inner life.

Having decided which animal you think is most like your character, find the means to observe this animal at a farm or a zoo, or research and find photographs that give you an idea of how the animal behaves. Practise imagining yourself as this animal and moving as the animal – you can then use this experience to build on the inner life of your character.

Task 2

Elements of costume can help you 'feel' more like the character. Try out a few of the following, depending on the kind of acting style required:

1 To help you be less modern and more formal in rehearsals:
- a collar that does up at the neck
- a belt that holds you in at the waist

- heeled shoes
- practice skirt

2 Hair – try your hair in different styles and find one that makes you feel less like you and more like the character.

3 Hats – always full of character, hats can help you with style, as can a walking stick.

Try out some of the above suggestions in rehearsals once you are off the book and want to feel like the character and not yourself.

Task 3

A prop often has a meaning that goes beyond everyday use and can be used to reflect how your character is feeling.

1 Props involving activity – for example, knitting, spinning, digging. These are part of the rhythm of the scene. Practise one of the activities while rehearsing your lines – use different emotions such as fear or anger while using the prop and note the difference this makes to your delivery.

2 If your scene calls for the use of props, you should practise as soon as possible. In order to get used to talking and carrying out an activity at the same time, you could try the following:
- Recite your lines in the play while making a cup of tea/coffee – try to concentrate and if you 'fluff' the lines go back and start again.
- Recite your lines whilst getting dressed in the morning.
- Get the other people to recite their lines with you whilst eating your lunch.

ACTIVITY 9

The following tasks can be used to help you create your own characters to use in improvisations and role-plays. They will also help to give you further information that is not included in a text. You should do this exercise as your character – answering the questions as your character would.

Task 1

Hot-seating

Do this exercise with a partner who will also be in character.

Starter questions to ask each other:
- What is your name?
- How old are you?
- Where do you live?
- Do you have any family?
- Do you have a job?
- Who are your friends?
- What are your interests?

Follow-up questions to ask each other:
- What are your likes?
- What are your dislikes?
- What makes you happy?
- What do you think the future holds for you?
- Are you afraid of anything?
- What was the worst moment in your life?
- What was the best moment in your life?

After you have both finished asking these questions, discuss what you have learned about your characters.

Task 2

Status

Knowing the status of the character you are playing makes your acting easier and more natural. Remembering that the conditions of status are to do with **position**, **personal** and **social**, try to find some other examples for the lists below:

Status		
HIGHER	EQUAL	LOWER
Monarch	All being knighted together	About to receive knighthood
Bank manager		
Head teacher		
		Shop assistant
	Politicians – back benches	

Task 3

Bearing in mind that you can show the change of status by eye contact, body language, vocal quality and behaviour, try the following exercise with a partner:

With another student, start off an ordinary conversation about your journey to college/school today – as you are talking to each other, keep changing your status.

For example:

One moment you could be very confidently shouting your information over the top of your partner because of your **high** status and the next moment you could be very quiet and not say a lot and look at the floor because of your **low** status.

Do this for about five minutes, then stop and discuss what means you both used to change the status and how that made you feel. Now go back to the character you are playing and make some decisions as to what status you think your character is at various times in the drama.

ACTIVITY 10

At the start of the rehearsal period always think about the following questions:

1 Where have you come from?
2 Where are you going?
3 Why are you there?

It is always useful to know your character's objective for the whole play, ie what you want to have achieved by the end of the play.

Task 1

If you are studying a naturalistic text, use your script and all of the activities and answer the following seven questions:

Who am I?

eg name, age, sex, race, occupation, social class

Where am I?

eg location, date, country

When am I?

eg time, era, political/religious context, how does time affect me? What am I allowed to do?

What do I want?

eg action, objective, super-objective

What is my obstacle?

How am I going to get what I want?

What am I physically going to have to do to get what I want?

What do I want?

What is my motivation?

Task 2

Make decisions in a column:

Similarities to you	Differences to you

ACTIVITY 11

FINDING YOUR FOCUS WHEN DEVISING

Within your group discussions for a devised piece, ask yourselves the following questions:

1 **What** and **why** (what do you want to say about the topic and why should an audience want to know about it)?

2 **Who** are the important characters?

3 **Where** is the piece set?

4 **When** (the timeline of your story, the cause and effect)?

For a group-devised piece to be successful you must have clear answers to these four questions that you all agree on!

For example:

In our group discussion we decided on bullying as a topic for our devised piece of drama. To help us focus we asked ourselves the following questions:

1 WHAT and WHY

We decided that we would focus our topic of bullying on our own peer group as we felt that our audience would be able to relate to that.

2 WHO

The important characters in our piece will be two girls called Sarah and Emma who are bullying a boy called James. We chose these characters as we felt it would be harder for a boy to confess that he was being bullied than it would be for a girl.

3 WHERE

The drama will be set in the college canteen. We decided on this setting because we felt that the bullying would not be noticed by other students so much if there were lots of people around.

4 WHEN

We decided the action would take place at 3.30 pm during the afternoon break for most classes. This would add to the drama as it would be nearly time to go home and James would have to face going with the bullies on the bus.

ACTIVITY 12

In your groups, using your topic from Activity 11, try out the following six tasks that introduce different ways of improvising to help find a style to your piece.

Task 1

Movement with narrator

Have a person as a narrator who tells the story in the third person while the others in the group mime the actions.

Task 2

Cutting the language down

Ask each person in the group to write down two sentences which most strongly show the feelings of their character. Then use these sentences as the only form of words you can use in the improvisation – you can split them up, change the order round and repeat them as often as you would like.

Task 3

Movement alone

Improvise the scene with no words at all, seeing if you can make it clear to the people watching. You could use a drum or music to help.

Task 4

Specialised style

Turn your improvisation into a fairy story or a musical with song and dance.

Task 5

Changing the location or time

Improvise your scene in an entirely different place and time – remember to use a time and place where the events might have happened.

Task 6

Changing the frame

Choose one person to tell the story as if it is being told to a psychiatrist. Use flashbacks so that the others in your group re-enact what has been said.

ACTIVITY 13

Below are some tips for helping you to memorise your lines. Not all of them will work for you as everyone is different, but try them out and select one that will work best for you.

It is a good idea to highlight your speeches with a highlighter pen: this makes your lines stand out and also makes it easier to find your place when using your script in rehearsals.

Practising at home

Task 1

Give your script to a friend or parent and get them to read out the last sentence that comes before each of your lines. This is called cueing. Listen for the key word in the cue, which will help you to remember when to speak.

Task 2

Record the other actor's lines, leaving a blank space for you to say your line after hearing your cue. Play back the recording without looking at your script and see if you can fill in the blanks.

Task 3

Repetition is always good. Say the words out loud in order to feel the words pass through your vocal chords and hear what you are saying and this way you will remember what you are saying more easily. Say your lines over and over again out loud and you are less likely to freeze during rehearsals.

Long speeches – be patient!

Task 4

Learn the speech line by line – go as far as you can and if you forget just look up the next three or four words and start at the beginning again. Remember to practise this out loud.

Task 5

Go over your lines just before you go to sleep at night and then shortly after getting up in the morning, then test yourself to see how much you remember. As the brain is active at night, it can remember what you read before you sleep.

Movement

Task 6

Words in a speech can remind you of a movement. Set up tables and chairs at home to represent the arrangement of furniture in your stage setting. Then walk through your part as you memorise it.

With a partner

Task 7

One of you can act as the coach with the script while the other actor practises the lines without a script. The coach can cue their partner if they need help. After five minutes swap over so that the actor now becomes the coach with the script.

ACTIVITY 14

INNER AND OUTER CHARACTERISTICS

This activity is to add to your character biography and can be used for scripted or unscripted work.

Task 1

Remembering that the definitions are as follows:

Inner characteristics
What your character really is

Outer characteristics
What your character appears to be

make yourself two headings and list the characteristics you begin to discover during the rehearsal period:

Inner	Outer
Brave	Reserved

Task 2

To get used to compiling these lists, use people you know really well such as parents, siblings or best friends. Think really hard about how well you know them and if what they appear to be to others is really what you think they are inside. Ask someone to do it for you and see if you agree.

ACTIVITY 15

REHEARSAL TECHNIQUES

Task 1

Some exercises you can do to help you concentrate:

1 When you are alone, concentrate on a specific memory that means something to you without allowing any other thoughts to invade and spoil it.

2 Work out a maths problem in your head.

3 Work out a personal problem in your head.

4 Have an argument in your head.

5 Read – people who read a lot are usually good at concentration.

6 Learn to talk well – making a connection between what you are thinking and the words you use. Choose a subject and talk out loud about it for thirty minutes – this should be continuous chatter until the words begin to flow out of you.

7 Remember – **Look**, **Listen**, **Read**, **Talk**.

Task 2

One of the hardest things for a young actor is to ensure that any movement around the stage looks natural and has purpose. Why and when should you move?

- Go through your script and look for things your character says that could have just occurred to them. This is a new thought that comes with new energy, which would make you want to move.

- Look in the direction you are going before you go, and the move will look and feel more natural. Practise looking down before you sit and looking up before you stand. People who are behaving naturally in the real world will want to make sure the chair is there before they go to sit down.

- Try moving slowly when you are speaking quickly and moving quickly when you are speaking slowly – difficult but it works.

- Look, move, speak – an exercise for this is to pretend that you are showing a prospective buyer around your home, pointing out its good and bad features and its contents. Be conscious of first looking at the thing, moving towards it and then speaking about it.

Task 3

When you have to go over and over things in rehearsals, it is very easy to lose your instinct and motivation. Here are a few exercises to help 'keep it real':

- Go through the whole of your part out loud while you are washing up but shout your lines as if you want someone in the next room to hear you.

- Instead of acting your part, sit in a chair and tell the story of the scenes to someone – use what you can remember of the other character's lines and include your own.

For example:

'So she arrives home and says, where have you been and I say that I have been here all the time. She looks very suspicious and asks me to tell her what I have been doing all this time. I madly try to think of any programmes on telly I could have been watching…'

ACTIVITY 16

USING YOUR IMAGINATION!

Use the following nursery rhyme for this activity:

> Mary had a little lamb
> Whose fleece was white as snow,
> And everywhere that Mary went
> The lamb was sure to go.
>
> It followed her to school one day,
> Which was against the rule;
> It made the children laugh and play
> To see the lamb at school.

Say the above in the following ways:

- as if you can't quite remember it and have only just learned it
- as a sermon in church
- as if to a foreigner with very little knowledge of English
- as if the lamb had just died
- as if Mary had just died
- as if you are a Sunday-school teacher talking to small children
- as if you are drunk

You can then try this with your own words, changing the meaning, in order to keep it fresh.

UNIT 49 – DEVELOPING MOVEMENT SKILLS

This section focuses on grading criteria P1, M1, D1, P2, M2, D2, P3, M3, D3, P4, M4, D4, P5, M5, D5.

Learning outcomes

1 Be able to execute movement actions
2 Know how to apply movement techniques and principles
3 Know how to use relationships in movement

Content

1) Execute movement actions

Travel: walking; running; triplets; prances; leaps; as a transition; with a partner; in a group; use of technique; stylistic differences; technical, pedestrian

Turns: rolls; spins; pirouettes; twist; pivot; isolated body parts, whole body turns

Elevation: hop; leap; jump; sissone; assemble; (1-1, 1 to the other, 2-2, 2-1,1-2); preparation; take off, landing

Gesture: functional; non-functional; conversational; social; emotional; shadowing speech

Stillness and falling: pause; shape; tableaux; use of centre to aid balance; on and off balance; suspension; fall and recovery

2) Techniques and principles

Spatial awareness: personal and general space; kinesphere, positive and negative space, body shape, projection; peripheral vision; proximity, relation to others, spatial boundaries in relation to audience; floor and air pattern; pathways; lines in space, curved, straight, circular, freeform, shape, group formation; direction; forwards, backwards, sideways, diagonal, up, down, stage directions; dimensions; plane and levels, height, width, depth, vertical, horizontal, sagittal, low, middle, high

Dynamic principles: effort; punch, slash, wring, press, float, glide, dab, flick; time; sudden, sustained; weight; firm, light; space; direct, flexible; flow; bound, free

Timing: principles of time; duration, tempo, rhythm, accent, counterpoint; performing; phrasing, phrase length, counting, accuracy, musical/visual cues

3) Relationships in movement

Physical: group shape; interaction; improvising; trust work; weight bearing; lifting; carrying; tableaux

Grading criteria

P1 execute movement actions accurately most of the time

This means you will be able to carry out [execute] movement actions such as travelling, turns, elevations, gestures, stillness and falling correctly with precision [accurately] most of the time.

M1 execute movement actions accurately with a sense of competence and control

To achieve a Merit, you will perform the movement actions correctly and with precision [accurately], while demonstrating complete control over these movements.

D1 execute movement actions accurately with confidence and attention to detail

Distinction students will also perform with confidence, noticing, correcting and ensuring that every movement, however small, is correct and precise.

P2 show some understanding of spatial awareness

This means that you have demonstrated the ability to move with insight and basic interpretation, being aware of the space in which you move.

M2 demonstrate spatial awareness in a considered way and with an awareness of how to relate body movements to it

To achieve a Merit, you will have performed, showing that your spatial awareness is carefully thought out [considered] and how your body movements (large, small, travelling, stillness, etc) connect [relate] with your use of space.

D2 demonstrate spatial awareness in an assured manner and manipulate it effectively, with dramatic outcome

Distinction students will be confident and use spatial awareness skills creatively within performance, to benefit the drama and quality of the dance piece.

P3 show some understanding of elementary dynamic principles

This means that you have demonstrated insight and basic [elementary] interpretation [understanding] of dynamic principles within movement.

M3 understand the application of dynamic principles and their effect on movement

To achieve a Merit, you will be able to demonstrate your understanding of dynamic principles practically through performance and show how these skills have changed and varied your movement.

D3 understand and apply dynamic principles with insight and imagination

Distinction students will also use dynamic principles within movement without thinking [intuitively and naturally], using the skills with creative inventiveness [imagination].

P4 move with some understanding of timing

This means that you have demonstrated the ability to move using timing techniques with some insight and interpretation and/or meaning [understanding].

M4 move with an effective understanding of the relationship between movement and time structures

To achieve a Merit, students will demonstrate that their understanding of timing has successfully produced a desired or intended result [effective understanding], showing connection and/or similarity between their movement and time structures.

D4 move with a thorough understanding of the relationship between movement and time structures

Distinction students' movement using time structures will show a complete and detailed understanding, carried out with care [thorough understanding].

P5 use some relationships in movement

This means you will have demonstrated a number of examples of good movement skills with other people, creating relationships between dancers.

M5 use relationships appropriately in relationship to theme/stimuli

To achieve a Merit, you will have worked with others using creative movement skills and a theme or other stimulus to influence your work.

D5 use relationships effectively to communicate and express theme/stimuli

To achieve a Distinction, you will have worked with others successfully to produce a desired result [effectively], communicating and expressing a theme or stimulus through the use of creative movement skills.

ACTIVITY 1

BASIC MOVEMENT EXERCISES

Developing movement skills is important to any performer, whether you are a dancer, a music theatre performer or an actor. This first activity covers the basics that will help you understand the rest of the activities and gets you warmed up.

Task 1

Music Counting

Play a music track of your choice (not too fast) and try these exercises:

- Simply clap in time with the music and practise counting in 8s:
  1 – 2 – 3 – 4 – 5 – 6 – 7 – 8
- Now clap to the music double time, add an 'and' in between each count of the beats: 1-&-2-&-3-&-4-&-5-&-6-&-7-&-8
- Now walk around the room in time to the music. Feel the beat:
  1 – 2 – 3 – 4 – 5 – 6 – 7 – 8
- Quicken your steps to double time:
  1-&-2-&-3-&-4-&-5-&-6-&-7-&-8
- Now run. Can you keep in time to the music?

Task 2

Moving through space

Spatial awareness is incredibly important in the performing arts. When working with movement (in dance, acting or musical theatre) performers must be aware of their personal space and the general space around them. Discovering creative ways to travel through space can help develop interesting choreographic ideas or help with the physicality of a character.

Start walking around the room and follow the instructions below:

- Walk forwards.
- Walk backwards.
- Walk sideways.
- Walk up high on the tips of your toes.
- Walk low with bent knees.
- Move through the room drawing curvy pathways with your arms and legs.
- In space, draw the letter 'S' with your body – draw the letter 'O' – draw a number '8'.
- Move through the room drawing straight pathways with straight movements.
- Move through the room drawing a zigzag pathway with your knees and elbows.
- Move through the room as slow as you possibly can.
- Move through the room as fast as you possibly can.

Task 3

Growing and melting

We can move our bodies many different ways on different levels. The body is divided into three sections: *low level space*, from toes to hips; *middle level space*, from hips to shoulders; and *high level space*, everything above shoulders. Using different levels helps with general dynamics, enhancing choreography and movement onstage. The use of levels can also declare characters' status onstage, giving one performer more power than another, simply by their use of levels in their movement.

Start on the floor in a little ball and follow these instructions:

- Slowly uncurl your body and move continuously up until you are standing. Think about the idea of a flower growing and blooming: from a little seed to a fully matured plant.
- Now reverse the process. Start standing and move to the floor like an ice cube melting in the sun.
- Use your entire body. See what interesting shapes and movements you can achieve. Stretch your imagination and see how creative you can be with your ideas.

ACTIVITY 2

LEADING WITH A BODY PART

A musician uses an instrument to make music. A painter uses paint and a brush to create a painting. A writer uses a pen and paper or a computer to create a story. Likewise, a performer uses his/her body to create movement! Sometimes movements are full-bodied and sometimes they isolate just one or two body parts. The following activity will help you think about using different body parts to expand your creativity and your range of movements.

For each of the body parts listed below, let that part lead you through space.

For each body part, ask yourself: how does it feel to move around a room leading with that body part? Make your own version of the chart and write, in the appropriate spaces, what emotion might correspond with initiating your movement this way.

Right Arm   Left Leg

Emotion: _____   Emotion: _____

Left Elbow   Right Toes

Emotion: _____   Emotion: _____

Right Hip	Chest
Emotion: _____	Emotion: _____
Lower Back	Top of the Head
Emotion: _____	Emotion: _____
Right Wrist	Left Ear
Emotion: _____	Emotion: _____
Chin	Right Shoulder
Emotion: _____	Emotion: _____

If you were developing a performance role, how could initiating movements with different body parts help physicalise your character?

Imagine you need to play a very young child.

Which body part would initiate your movement?

ACTIVITY 3

OBSERVING BODY LANGUAGE

We use body language in our everyday lives to make silent, intuitive statements. Sometimes we are not even aware we are doing it. If we don't like someone and don't want to speak to them, we can move our body in a way that the person senses our attitude and doesn't approach us. If we are happy to speak to someone, our body movements are considerably different, inviting them to approach us.

Go to your town centre, high street or a busy shopping centre. Observe five people, male and female, young and old. Look at how they move. What does their body language say about them?

1 Describe what mood you think the person is in, ie happy, sad, angry, confused, etc.

2 What part of their body are they initiating their movements from? Do they walk leading with their pelvis? Are their shoulders slumped forward? Do they have a bounce in their step?

3 Describe how you might change their movement initiations to change their emotional mood.

Now try it yourself. Walk with your shoulders slumped forward and your knees bent. Answer the following questions:

1 How does this make your body feel?

2 What emotions does this signify for you?

3 Does walking this way affect your emotional state?

Walk rigidly with your shoulders pushed back. Keep your legs and arms extremely straight. Hold your head erect.

1 How does this make your body feel?

2 What emotions does this signify for you?

3 Does walking this way affect your emotional state?

Skip, letting your body be loose like wet noodles. Don't hold anything tight.

1 How does this make your body feel?

2 What emotions does this signify for you?

3 Does walking this way affect your emotional state?

ACTIVITY 4

SHAPES

Creating different shapes through movement can be an interesting exploration of your body's capabilities. Our bodies are constructed almost exactly symmetrically (having the parts of one side corresponding with those of the other) – two arms, two legs, etc. Yet we have the ability to make shapes not only symmetrically, but asymmetrically (not bilaterally symmetrical) as well.

Task 1

Find three objects from around your house – for example, a jar, a chair, a toothbrush, etc. Choose objects with varying shapes and sizes. Draw these objects on a piece of paper.

Task 2

Create a shape with your body representing each object.

Think about your use of levels. Is your object round or straight? Long or short? Smooth edges or rough edges?

Photograph your body shape for each of the three objects, print the photographs (on a computer) and paste them under the pictures you drew.

Task 3

Now create a movement that is an extension of your body shape.

For example, if your object is a jar and you create a round shape, low to the ground, your movement might be a rolling movement.

Use turns and elevation steps to create your travelling movement.

Create a mind-map describing each of your objects, shapes and movements. Stretch your imagination. What words can you come up with to describe your images?

For example:

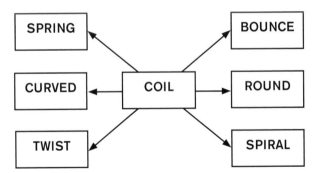

Task 4

Create a floor pattern for your object. How would it move in space? A straight line? Continuous spiralling loops? A zigzag? Draw the floor pattern for each of the three objects.

ACTIVITY 5

TABLEAUX

Using tableaux in performance pieces is an effective way to set a scene. It gives the audience time to see each character, the relationships between characters and what the whole scene is about. It creates a clear image for the audience to grab onto before the action begins. It can also give the audience a moment to process the current action within a scene, musical number or dance piece.

93

Select an image from, for example, a magazine postcard or newspaper that includes a variety of people with different relationships.

Describe each character in the picture.

What is their emotional state?

What are they thinking?

What is their relationship to the rest of the characters in the picture?

What is the overall image trying to convey? Is it successful?

Now describe how each character in the picture would move. Are they old and slow? Are they young and speedy?

Using the relationships between the characters and their juxtaposition in the picture, come up with a tableaux idea that would be the beginning image for a dance piece.

What would the lighting be like?

Where on stage would they be positioned?

What type of music would you use?

What would the content of the dance piece include?

ACTIVITY 6

BALANCE

Counterbalance

When pulling a very heavy object, do you lean towards it or away from it?
Counterbalance means a force or influence that equally counteracts another to achieve balance. Dancers and physical theatre actors counterbalance each other to create seemingly impossible and breathtaking physical shapes. In terms of safety, counterbalance tends to be riskier, because you are taking your weight away from your partner(s).

Contra-balance

Contra-balance means the application of two forces pushing together, applying equal levels of energy to support the physical body in space. As dancers and physical theatre actors use counterbalance, so do they use contra-balance to create physically difficult shapes. Contra-balance is a safer form of balancing because you are gaining more support from your partner(s).

- Think about the following three architectural sites:

   The Leaning Tower of Pisa

   The Sydney Opera House

   The Millennium Bridge

- Brainstorm ideas about how balance contributes to the success of each site.

- Now recreate each of these pieces of architecture with your body, focusing on the ideas of balance.

As you are creating these shapes by yourself, you will be using counterbalance in your own body.

1   What body parts are counterbalancing each other?

Now get a partner and, again, recreate these architectural sites with your bodies. Think about using both counterbalance and contra-balance.

2   Are you using counterbalance or contra-balance?

3   What body parts are counterbalancing each other?

4   What body parts are contra-balancing each other?

ACTIVITY 7

PHRASE ACCUMULATION

When choreographing and creating movement, it is not always necessary to continually make up new movement phrases. Using theme and variation gives a piece continuity and is an effective technique. A short movement phrase can be manipulated to create a much longer, more complex and visually interesting piece of choreography.

Create 8 non-locomotor movements and accumulate these movements to make a longer movement phrase:

1 – 1,2 – 1,2,3 – 1,2,3,4 – 1,2,3,4,5 – 1,2,3,4,5,6 – 1,2,3,4,5,6,7 – 1,2,3,4,5,6,7,8 – 2,3,4,5,6,7,8 – 3,4,5,6,7,8 – 4,5,6,7,8 – 5,6,7,8 – 6,7,8 – 7,8 – 8

ACTIVITY 8

PHONE NUMBERS

Create 10 movements and number them 0 to 9.

Task 1

Ask three people (friends, family and/or classmates) for their phone numbers:

Phone Number A _____

Phone Number B _____

Phone Number C _____

Accumulate your individual movements into phrases in the order of each phone number.

Task 2

Evaluate this activity.

- Describe your experience of creating these movement phrases. How easy or difficult did you find this exercise?
- Analyse the effectiveness of this exercise.
- What can you take from this exercise to apply to your future movement work?

ACTIVITY 9

MIRRORING

Task 1

Look in a mirror and move in smooth, slow, fluid movements.

- What observations can you make about your reflected movements?
- What are the important features of your movement, necessary to recreate the idea of a reflected image?

Task 2

Now, with a partner, stand facing each other, as if you're looking in a mirror at your own reflection. Pick one leader and one reflection.

- The leader now moves in smooth, slow, fluid movements and the reflection mirrors these movements.
- Reflection – try and follow the leader simultaneously, rather than being slightly behind.
- Switch roles.

Task 3

Now ask someone (friend, family member, classmate) to observe you and your partner and try and determine who is the leader and who is the reflection.

■ How successful were you at hiding who was the leader and who was the reflection?

■ What was challenging about this exercise?

■ What was easy about this exercise?

■ How does this exercise improve your knowledge of movement?

ACTIVITY 10

This activity involves understanding locomotor and non-locomotor movements.

Locomotor movement
Movement that travels through space

Non-locomotor movement (axial movement)
Movement that moves around the axis of the body (the spine)

Task 1

If you have access to a photocopier, make a copy of the 'Word Cards' opposite and cut them up.

Task 2

■ Select two of the words and string them together to create a new movement.
For example:
Shake + Crawl = shaking crawl

■ Describe what type of character might use this movement.
For example:
An old woman might use a shaking crawl. (Be inventive!)

Task 3

Devise a short scene around this character, using his/her movement (a shaking crawl). The story can be told completely through movement or using text. The scene must have a problem/conflict and a solution.

■ Where does the scene take place?

■ What characters are involved?

■ What is the scenario of the scene?

■ Describe the problem/conflict.

■ How is this problem/conflict resolved?

ACTIVITY 11

Do you ever meet someone and feel they are invading your 'personal space'? If they just took a step backwards, you'd feel much better. But to put your arm around your mum, dad, grandmother or grandfather feels comfortable. Why is that? Try exploring this idea with the following activity and see if you can make any conclusions about personal space vs. general space. As a performer, you will be required to use both personal space and general space and sometimes will need to let someone whom you don't know very well into your personal space and create the illusion that your relationship is very close. Can you succeed in this task?

With a partner, stand back to back.

Take one generous-sized step away from each other and turn to face each other.

Word Cards with locomotor and non-locomotor movements

Perform the actions and tick the boxes in each case.

WALK ❏ locomotor word or ❏ non-locomotor word?	**FALL** ❏ locomotor word or ❏ non-locomotor word?
STRETCH ❏ locomotor word or ❏ non-locomotor word?	**GALLOP** ❏ locomotor word or ❏ non-locomotor word?
RUN ❏ locomotor word or ❏ non-locomotor word?	**MELT** ❏ locomotor word or ❏ non-locomotor word?
BEND ❏ locomotor word or ❏ non-locomotor word?	**SLIDE** ❏ locomotor word or ❏ non-locomotor word?
SLITHER ❏ locomotor word or ❏ non-locomotor word?	**SWAY** ❏ locomotor word or ❏ non-locomotor word?
TWIST ❏ locomotor word or ❏ non-locomotor word?	**CREEP** ❏ locomotor word or ❏ non-locomotor word?
SKIP ❏ locomotor word or ❏ non-locomotor word?	**SHAKE** ❏ locomotor word or ❏ non-locomotor word?
SWING ❏ locomotor word or ❏ non-locomotor word?	**CRAWL** ❏ locomotor word or ❏ non-locomotor word?
HOP ❏ locomotor word or ❏ non-locomotor word?	**LUNGE** ❏ locomotor word or ❏ non-locomotor word?
PUSH ❏ locomotor word or ❏ non-locomotor word?	**SPIN** ❏ locomotor word or ❏ non-locomotor word?
JUMP ❏ locomotor word or ❏ non-locomotor word?	**CURL** ❏ locomotor word or ❏ non-locomotor word?
PULL ❏ locomotor word or ❏ non-locomotor word?	**RACE** ❏ locomotor word or ❏ non-locomotor word?
LEAP ❏ locomotor word or ❏ non-locomotor word?	**CONTRACT** ❏ locomotor word or ❏ non-locomotor word?
JOG ❏ locomotor word or ❏ non-locomotor word?	**BOUNCE** ❏ locomotor word or ❏ non-locomotor word?
FLOAT ❏ locomotor word or ❏ non-locomotor word?	**PUNCH** ❏ locomotor word or ❏ non-locomotor word?

■ For each card perform the action in bold on it and make a note of whether it is a
locomotor or non-locomotor movement.

1 Do you feel comfortable at this distance?

2 If playing a character on stage, what relationship might these two actors/dancers have?

3 How is this determined through their (the characters') use of space?

Take another two generous-sized steps away from each other.

1 Again, do you feel comfortable at this distance?

2 What relationship might your characters have and why?

Repeat: Take another two generous-sized steps away from each other and repeat the questions.

ACTIVITY 12

MOVEMENT MAPS

When creating movement on a stage, we make pathways with our feet and our whole body. We create different pathways through general space or can use body parts to create pathways moving through our personal space. Pathways can create complexity to movement phrases or can create relationships between characters.

Task 1

- On a blank piece of paper, draw three shapes (square, circle etc).
- Connect the three shapes with three different styles of lines (eg a zigzag line, a spiralling line, a straight line etc).
- Using the shapes and lines drawn on the paper as a 'map', create a movement phrase that travels in space, according to the pathways created on your 'map'.

The shapes on your 'map' should influence your movement choices (non-locomotor movements) and the 'map' itself should influence where in space you travel (locomotor movements).

For example:

A square might indicate sharp, angular movements.

A spiralling line might indicate smooth, round and turning travelling steps.

Imagine you are on stage in front of an audience. Think about projection and performance quality, as well as attention to timing, spacing and movement qualities.

Think about your use of levels and directions.

1 Were your movements gestural or full-bodied?

2 How did your 'map' influence your movement choices?

3 Was it easy or difficult to physically demonstrate your 'map'? Describe your process.

Task 2

Now work with a partner and repeat the exercise, but this time create a 'map' for each other.

1 Was it easier or more difficult to physicalise someone else's 'map'?

2 How well do you feel your partner followed his/her 'map'?

3 Where could improvements be made?

Give your partner feedback.

ACTIVITY 13

SPEED (PHRASING)

Timing is an important factor to consider when creating or executing movement. When you watch a film on DVD, you watch it at normal speed, but if you want to skip ahead to a later section of the film you can fast-forward the scenes. If you want to see a small detail, you can slow the scene down and watch it in slow motion. We can do the same with our own body movements and move at different speeds, from very fast to very slow. Speed can create intensity, dynamics and visual complexity in your movement phrases, helping to strengthen your overall performance.

Task 1

Create a 16-count phrase of movement. You can use music to inspire you and help you maintain your rhythm.

- Slow your phrase down to half-time, so every movement takes twice as long. This should now become a 32-count phrase of movement.
- Now speed your original 16-count phrase up to double-time, so every movement takes half as long. This should now become an 8-count phrase of movement.
- Put all three phrases together: normal speed, half-time and double-time. All this should now become a 56-count phrase of movement.

Task 2

Ask yourself these questions on the piece you have just constructed:

1 How do the dynamics of your movements change with varying speeds?
2 How can varying the speed of your movement create complexities within your choreography?

Now repeat this 56-count phrase standing in front of a mirror.

1 Do all three phrases, in varying speeds, look the same?
2 Which speed do you prefer the look of? Is it the original or do you prefer your variations?
3 Which speed is the hardest to execute?
4 Which speed is the easiest to execute?

ACTIVITY 14

MUSIC OBSERVATION

Task 1

Pick three of your favourite songs, of contrasting styles and speeds. Copy and complete the following table:

Name of song:	
Artist:	
Musical style and tempo:	
Name of song:	
Artist:	
Musical style and tempo:	
Name of song:	
Artist:	
Musical style and tempo:	

Task 2

Try to answer these questions:

1 What is the emotional feeling of each song?
2 How does the speed of the song help illustrate the song's emotional feeling?

Improvise movement to each song.

ACTIVITY 15

RHYTHM (POETRY)

Rhythm is a pattern of flow or movement. Your heart beats at a constant rhythm – a steady beat. You normally walk in an even rhythm as well. However, if you injure your ankle, for instance, and cannot put much weight on it, your walking rhythm becomes uneven as you take more time to step on your healthy ankle and less time to put weight onto your injured ankle. In movement, varying your rhythm and choosing different movements or beats to accent can make your phrase more interesting and is a good choreographic tool.

Look at the poem below, *The Owl and the Pussy-Cat* by Edward Lear.

Read through these first two verses a few times to get a sense of the rhythm of the poem.

The Owl and the Pussy-cat went to sea
In a beautiful pea green boat,
They took some honey, and plenty of money,
Wrapped up in a five pound note.
The Owl looked up to the stars above,
And sang to a small guitar,
'O lovely Pussy! O Pussy my love,
What a beautiful Pussy you are,
   You are,
   You are!
What a beautiful Pussy you are!'

Pussy said to the Owl, 'You elegant fowl!
How charmingly sweet you sing!
O let us be married! too long we have tarried:
But what shall we do for a ring?'
They sailed away, for a year and a day,
To the land where the Bong-tree grows
And there in a wood a Piggy-wig stood
With a ring at the end of his nose,
   His nose,
   His nose,
With a ring at the end of his nose.

Task 1

Now count the rhythm as if it were music, counting 1 to 8.

For example, the first line would be counted as:

1 - & - a – 2 - & - a – 3 - & - 4

Make a table like the one on the next page to record your counts to the poem.

Task 2

Now create movement phrases using the rhythms from the table. Try to tell the poem's story through your movement.

1 Describe your experience of creating these movement phrases. How easy or difficult did you find this exercise?

2 Analyse the effectiveness of this exercise.

3 What can you take from this exercise to apply to your future movement work?

The Owl and the Pussy-cat went to sea
In a beautiful pea green boat,
They took some honey, and plenty of money,
Wrapped up in a five pound note.
The Owl looked up to the stars above,
And sang to a small guitar,
'O lovely Pussy! O Pussy my love,
What a beautiful Pussy you are,
You are,
You are!
What a beautiful Pussy you are!'
Pussy said to the Owl, 'You elegant fowl!
How charmingly sweet you sing!
O let us be married! too long we have tarried:
But what shall we do for a ring?'
They sailed away, for a year and a day,
To the land where the Bong-tree grows
And there in a wood a Piggy-wig stood
With a ring at the end of his nose,
His nose,
His nose,
With a ring at the end of his nose.

ACTIVITY 16

TRUST WORK

With a partner, choose a 'Person A' and a 'Person B'.

Task 1

- Person B stands behind Person A.
- Person A falls backwards, like an ironing board, and Person B catches their weight, supporting Person A on their back (at their shoulder blades).
- Start very small and slowly increase the distance between Person A and Person B.
- Now switch roles.

Task 2

Now Person A becomes a lump of clay and Person B becomes a sculptor.

- Person B moulds Person A into various shapes.
- Think creatively. Use levels. Use curved shapes. Use angular shapes.
- Think about arms, legs, torso, head, fingers, toes. What facial expressions can you give your clay?
- Now switch roles.

Task 3

Now work with your partner moving across a room. Start at one end of the room and try to move together to the other side of the room without losing contact – some part of your bodies must ALWAYS be touching.
Move slowly and deliberately and work together to create your movements. Be creative!
Repeat this exercise, but work on going beyond staying in contact with your partner

and work on actually sharing weight. Can you trust your partner to support you? Can your partner trust you? Do you make him/her feel at ease? Stretch your creativity and work together as a unit.

MARKED ASSIGNMENTS

UNIT 3 – THE PERFORMING ARTS BUSINESS

UNIT 4 – THE HISTORICAL CONTEXT OF PERFORMANCE

UNIT 20 – APPLYING ACTING STYLES

UNIT 54 – CANCE APPRECIATION

Unit 3: The Performing Arts Business

Assignment Sheet

The Imaginary High School
Music & Performing Arts Department
National Certificate in Performing Arts

Student Name:		Student Number:	

Assignment Title:	Finance budget for regional children's play

Assessor:	Richard Hart	Assignment Ref:	03-Budget01

Date Set:	1st February	Completion Date:	18th March

Unit Number	Unit Title	Criteria Covered
3	The Performing Arts Business	4

Scenario

You are a producer in a small independent theatre company based outside London. Your Managing Director has managed to convince an old friend and an experienced 'theatre angel' to invest in a new touring production for the company. You have been asked to prepare a budget for a production for Roald Dahl's Fantastic Mr Fox adapted by Sally Reid. You have been given a copy of the script to help costing the show and you will need to choose a suitable regional theatre for the show to run for 4 weeks during the summer.

Grading Criteria

UNIT		Pass		Merit		Distinction
3	P4	prepare a production budget for a performing arts event that addresses the essential areas of income and expenditure	M4	prepare a production budget for a performing arts event that addresses most of the relevant areas of income and expenditure with meaningful figures	D4	prepare a budget for a performing arts event that is comprehensive and accurate based on careful research

Task		Action	Criteria	Completed
1.	Research your production	<ul><li>Read through the script, making notes on cast size, costumes, set etc.</li><li>Decide on a suitable regional theatre for your 4 week run of this play for children</li><li>Make notes of anything that might affect your approach to producing this play and costings; e.g. the play does not have an interval – how will this affect your budget?</li></ul>	Unit 3 P4, M4, D4	

104

Task		Action	Criteria	Completed
2.	Research your costings	Good research will mean that your budget can be more accurate. Some items will be very difficult for you to guess without years of experience (e.g. set construction), try breaking these elements down further to help you give your best guess (e.g. wood, paint, screws, wages)	Unit 3 P4, M4, D4	
3.	Prepare your budget	• Present your budget using a spreadsheet and use calculations to give totals. Make sure you are clear about what includes or does not include VAT. • Ensure that you include: Capital & Running Costs and Income • The budget should also include a balance sheet	Unit 3 P4, M4, D4	
4.	Explanation of items	Ensure you have detailed explanations, where necessary, to help explain your budget.	Unit 3 P4, M4, D4	
5.	Bibliography, resource list	Make sure you include at the end any websites, publications, phone calls and books detailing where you obtained the information.		
6.	Final deadline **18th March @ 3.30pm**	All budgets should be handed in to the performing arts administration office by 3.30pm		

N.B. This assignment does not complete the assessment of this unit or the individual criteria targeted within this assignment. Students will have to successfully complete at least another two assignments during the course to meet the requirements of the unit.

PASS LEVEL ANSWER

UNIT 3: THE PERFORMING ARTS BUSINESS
BRET

Budget – Fantastic Mr Fox Children's Show

Costs	Wages & Fees	Director	£10,000	
		Actors	£190,000	
		Stage Management	£15,000	
	Set Design		£2,000	
	Lighting		£500	
	Sound		£500	
	Costume		£1,500	
	Props		£200	
	Rehearsal Space		£800	
	Performance Space		£4,000	
	Publicity & Marketing		£10,000	
	Transport		£500	TOTAL
	Royalities		£5,000	£240,000

Income	Tickets	£192,000	
	Programmes	£10,000	
	Grants	£10,000	
	Sponsorship	£20,000	
	Workshops	£8,000	TOTAL
	Special Events	£2,500	£242,500

BALANCE	£2,500

Budget Explanation – Fantastic Mr Fox Children's Show

COSTS

Wages & Fees

The rehearsals go on for 6 weeks and the 4 weeks of performances. I have paid the Director £1000 a week, Actors £500 and Stage Managers £300. I have calculated for 38 actors as this is what the script said and 5 stage managers to sort lighting, sound and the set.

Set Design, Lighting, Sound, Costume, Props

I have estimated how much it would cost to make the set or hire things.

Rehearsal Space

Needed for 6 weeks of rehearsals, The local church said that I could hire their hall during the week for £200 each week, however I would ask for a further discount for booking six weeks, which makes £800.

Performance Space

I went on the website for a local theatre that has 400 seats and it said that you could hire it for £1000 a week × 4 weeks

Publicity & marketing

I want to get lots of people to know about my show and so I will advertise in papers, put lots of posters up and print leaflets. I thought about employing people to hand out leaflets on the streets as the town gets really busy. We have two local radio stations that are both rubbish, but some mothers might listen to it, so I will pay to advertise on them.

Transport

In case anyone needs to move things around

Royalities

I have budgeted £5000 for royalities

INCOME

Ticket sales

I had to go to the ballet with school and tickets cost £28 each and it was rubbish and I thought really expensive, so I thought I could easily charge £20, I don't think people will complain about the price as I have more people in my show. £20 × 400 seats, and I plan to have 6 performances each week.

Programmes

I will sell programmes for £2 each and I have estimated that I will sell programmes to at least 50% of the audience.

Grants/Sponsorships

As this is a kids show and its very expensive to run with such a big cast, I will apply for funding from the Arts Council and approach local businesses to sponsor the show. I will target businesses that are involved with children in some way so they see that they are advertising too.

Workshops/Special events

I thought the actors could do some workshops and other events during the day that we could charge to local schools and youth clubs.

ASSESSOR FEEDBACK FORM

Assessment Feedback Sheet

The Imaginary High School – Music & Performing Arts Department

National Certificate in Performing Arts

Learner's Name:	Bret	Student Number:	60481

Assignment Title:	Finance budget for regional children's play

Assessor:	Richard Hart	Assignment Ref:	03-Budget01

Date Set:	1st February	Completion Date:	18th March

Unit Number	Unit Title	Criteria Covered
3	The Performing Arts Business	4

Evidence for assessment complete?	YES		Is this a Final Assessment?	YES	
Is this an Interim Assessment?		NO	Can the student re-submit?	YES	

Assessment

Unit		Pass			Merit	
3	P4	prepare a production budget for a performing arts event that addresses the essential areas of income and expenditure	✓	M4	prepare a production budget for a performing arts event that addresses most of the relevant areas of income and expenditure with meaningful figures	
		Distinction		**Assessor's Comment**		
	D4	prepare a budget for a performing arts event that is comprehensive and accurate based on careful research		You have prepared a simple budget that does cover the main areas of income and expenditure. However, it is clear that you have simply got the list of items from out of the unit specification with little thought on how they apply to this particular production. Therefore this budget lacks specific, meaningful and sometimes relevant figures which demonstrates a lack of research.		

Assessor's General Comments

Bret, I have outlined below some actions to improve your work for next time or in case you wish to re-submit this particular assignment. Please read carefully as these pointers will also help you understand how to think like a producer.

Make sure you research properly. For example:

- Wages for your director are way too high for this kind of production
- Members of the technical team would usually get at least the same as the actors

You did not think to try and reduce the cast, no professional production would have 38 actors, especially a children's show. Proper study of the script would make a producer see the potential of actors doubling.

You have budgeted for lighting, sound and set but it is way too low. If you have 38 actors all needing a costume and divide £1500 between the number of actors, each costume has to only cost £40 to make, this might cover materials but nowhere have you budgeted for the people making or designing the costumes, which is also reflected in the areas of lighting/sound/props.

INCOME – although I agree that you are under-cutting the ballet, have you researched the usual cost of going to a children's show that only lasts an hour? It would cost two parents with three kids £100 to see your show, they simply would not be able to afford it. This is especially a concern when your budget relies on selling every ticket.

Hopefully you can recognise the depth in which you need to go to access Merit and Distinction grades. Remember that when you write an essay you have to justify every comment you make, in a budget you have to be able to justify every figure you have written down. Would you feel comfortable to stand up in front of the 'theatre angel' and present these figures, let alone be questioned? Would you dare to go on Dragon's Den with this kind of preparation? Although you would have made great TV, I don't think you would want to face their criticism, so please spend more time on your research.

Assessor's Name:	Richard Hart	Student's Name:	Bret
Assessor's Signature:		Student's Signature:	
Date:	21st March	Date:	23rd March

UNIT 3: THE PERFORMING ARTS BUSINESS
DAN

Fantastic Mr Fox – Budget

Capital Costs – 1 Week

Director's Fees	£2,300.00
Designer's Fees	£2,300.00
Lighting Designer's Fees	£1,000.00
Production Manager (£400 per week)	£400.00
Producer (£500 per week)	£500.00
26 × Actors (£300 per week each)	£7,800.00
4 × Stage Managers (£300 per week each)	£1,200.00
Set/Props	£10,000.00
Costumes	£6,000.00
Theatre Hire for Rehearsals (per week)	£12,000.00
Leaflets (40,000 × DLs)	£800.00
Posters (200 × A3)	£300.00
General Administration Costs	£400.00
Total	**£45,000.00**

Running Costs – 4 Weeks

Production Manager (£400 per week)	£1,600.00
Producer (£500 per week)	£2,000.00
26 × Actors (£300 per week each)	£31,200.00
4 × Stage Managers (£300 per week each)	£4,800.00
Theatre Hire for performances	£48,000.00
Wardrobe Running Costs	£400.00
Props Running Costs	£200.00
Lighting Running Costs	£1,200.00
Sound Running Costs	£1,200.00
Marketing & Advertising	£1,000.00
Total	**£91,600.00**

Income

Ticket Sales (£8 × 800 per show × 28 shows)	£179,200.00

Balance Sheet

Income	£179,200.00
Capital & Running Costs	£136,600.00
Balance	**£42,600.00**

Fantastic Mr Fox – Budget

Capital Costs

I plan to have one week of rehearsals for which the Director will get a set fee to direct and create the show with the actors and designers. The Designer (Set & Costume) and Lighting Designer also has a set fee for their work. The production manager is paid £400 per week as I thought he should get more than the actors, and the Producer is paid £500 a week (me) because I should get more than anyone because I am in charge.

The actors and stage managers are paid £300 per week, which is a sum in an example budget on the Arts Council website.

I thought the set and costumes would cost a lot to make and for materials, I looked on the B & Q website but it was really difficult to know exactly how much it would cost as I didn't really know what it would look like and how it would be made.

I have budgeted for hiring the theatre for the rehearsal week.

I decided to have DL sized leaflets printed and some posters. I got the price from a website for a printer nearby. I also thought that I might need some money for everyday things like photocopying, paper...

Running Costs

Production Manager, Producer, Actors and Stage Managers paid the same as rehearsal week but for the 4 performance weeks.

Theatre Hire stays the same but is multiplied by 4 weeks.

I budgeted for £100 a week for Wardrobe and £50 a week for Props, maybe if things get broken or ripped. If I needed to hire any extra lighting or sound I budgeted £300 a week for both.

I thought I would do some advertising in newspapers and on radio or even TV and therefore have £1000 for this.

Income

I thought I would charge £10 for adults and £6 for children, I therefore calculated my income on the average ticket price of £8. As The Palace Theatre is huge I never thought I would be able to fill it so I estimated that I would sell 800 seats rather than 1200 for each performance. I reckoned that I would get my cast to do 28 shows over the four weeks.

Balance

I am hoping if I sell enough tickets that will have an income of £179,200 and costs of £136,600 so I would make a profit of £42,600 which I think is great!

Websites: Arts Council, The Palace Theatre and Misc. Printers

ASSESSOR FEEDBACK FORM

Assessment Feedback Sheet

The Imaginary High School – Music & Performing Arts Department
National Certificate in Performing Arts

Learner's Name:	Dan	Student Number:	60348

Assignment Title:	Finance budget for regional children's play

Assessor:	Richard Hart	Assignment Ref:	03-Budget01

Date Set:	1st February	Completion Date:	18th March

Unit Number	Unit Title	Criteria Covered
3	The Performing Arts Business	4

Evidence for assessment complete?	YES		Is this a Final Assessment?	YES	

Is this an Interim Assessment?		NO	Can the student re-submit?	YES	

Assessment

Unit		Pass			Merit	
3	P4	prepare a production budget for a performing arts event that addresses the essential areas of income and expenditure	✓	M4	prepare a production budget for a performing arts event that addresses most of the relevant areas of income and expenditure with meaningful figures	✓
		Distinction			**Assessor's Comment**	
	D4	prepare a budget for a performing arts event that is comprehensive and accurate based on careful research			A good attempt to cover all budgetary aspects of this production. Although there are some gaps within the items listed, it is clear that for most of the time you have listed figures that are meaningful. More detailed research and accuracy within figures and their reason would have enabled you to achieve a Distinction.	

Assessor's General Comments

If you wish to re-submit the work for this assignment please consider the following to ensure that your budget demonstrates a thorough understanding of all the costs and income potential:

It is clear that you have researched salaries accurately from the Arts Council website; however, although the weekly fees are sensible you have not included any travel or accommodation fees for working at a regional theatre.

Although you have budgeted correctly for fewer actors than the script describes, nowhere have you indicated why and how you came to the conclusion of 26 actors. Therefore the reader and potential investor does not know whether this decision is an accident or from careful research and decision-making.

Why is the rehearsal period only a week and why are you rehearsing in a very expensive theatre? This demonstrates a lack of understanding of the production process. 26 actors will need a lot longer than a week to learn lines and block the show for a professional production. A large rehearsal room will be much cheaper than an entire theatre for this work.

Could you think of more potential avenues for income? What about programmes, merchandising, grants?

It is, however, a good attempt at a difficult task and your presentation is clear and professional.

Assessor's Name:	Richard Hart		**Student's Name:**	Dan
Assessor's Signature:			**Student's Signature:**	
Date:	21st March		**Date:**	23rd March

DISTINCTION LEVEL ANSWER

UNIT 3: THE PERFORMING ARTS BUSINESS
MADDY

Capital Costs

Salaries

notes	description	total each	no.	total
CC01	Actors	£1,200	16	£19,200
CC02	Assistant Stage Manager	£1,200	2	£2,400
CC03	Deputy Stage Manager	£1,500	1	£1,500
CC04	Company Stage Manager	£1,800	1	£1,800
			total	**£24,900**

Creative Fees

notes	description	total
CC05	Director	£2,500
CC06	Set/Costume Designer	£2,200
CC07	Lighting Designer	£1,000
CC08	Sound Designer	£1,000
CC09	Composer	£1,500
CC10	Production Manager	£2,500
CC11	Producer	£3,500
	total	**£14,200**

Rehearsal Costs

notes	description	total
CC12	Audition Costs	£1,000
CC13	Scripts/Copying	£500
CC14	Rehearsal Rooms	£3,760
CC15	Rehearsal Hires	£400
	total	**£5,660**

Production Costs

notes	description	total
CC16	Set Construction	£6,000
CC17	Props	£1,500
CC18	Costumes/Wigs	£8,000
CC19	Masks	£5,000
	total	**£20,500**

Marketing Costs

notes	description	total
CC20	Advertising	£1,600
CC21	FOH Displays	£300
CC22	Print	£1,800
CC23	Photographer	£400
	total	£4,100

General Administration

notes	description	total
CC24	Opening Night/Entertainment	£1,000
CC25	Get In/Out	£600
CC26	Transport	£300
	total	£1,900

	Total Capital Costs	**£71,260**

Income

notes	description	per week	no.	total
I01	Ticket Sales	£48,384	4	£193,536
I02	Programme Sales	£2,400	4	£9,600
I03	Mask Making Workshops	−£424	4	−£1,696
I04	Merchandising	£2,000	4	£8,000
I05	Local Authority Grant	£1,000	4	£4,000
			total	£213,440

Running Costs

Salaries

notes	description	total each	no.	total
RC01	Actors – Normal Minimum	£1,360	16	£21,760
RC02	Actors – Subsistence	£360	16	£5,760
RC03	Actors – Weekly Touring	£676	16	£10,816
RC04	Actors – Contingency			£5,000
RC05	ASM – Normal Minimum	£1,360	2	£2,720
RC06	ASM – Subsistence	£360	2	£720
RC07	ASM – Weekly Touring	£676	2	£1,352
RC08	DSM – Normal Minimum	£1,700	1	£1,700
RC09	DSM – Subsistence	£360	1	£360

Creative Fees

notes	description	each perf.	no.	total
RC14	Author/Adaptation	£90	48	£4,320
			total	**£4,320**

Production Costs

notes	description	per week	no.	total
RC15	Lighting Hire	£900	4	£3,600
RC16	Sound Hire	£500	4	£2,000
RC17	Misc Hire	£200	4	£800
RC18	Repairs	£150	4	£600
			total	**£7,000**

Marketing Costs

notes	description	total
RC19	Print	£600
RC20	Advertising	£3,000
	total	**£3,600**

	Total Running Costs	**£68,860**

Balance Sheet

notes	costs	total
B01	Capital	£71,260
B02	Running	£68,860
B03	total	£140,120
B04	+ 15%	£161,138

notes	income	total
B05	All income, excluding investors	**£213,440**

B06	**Balance**	**£52,302**

Notes – Fantastic Mr Fox Budget

CC01   A short play for children couldn't justify employing 38 actors. Having analysed the script carefully many of the smaller parts can be doubled with actors have quick costume changes. Some of the small children animals could even be played by hand puppets. I therefore decided I could employ just 16 actors and this would also give the production some slack if there were illnesses and lead parts had to be covered by understudies. Therefore Actors salaries have been calculated 16 actors rehearsing for 4 weeks at a London rehearsal venue (therefore no travel expenses required).
£300 (TMA Rehearsal Rate) × 4 (Rehearsal Weeks)

CC02   Assistant Stage Managers £300 (TMA Rehearsal Rate) × 4 (Rehearsal Weeks)
ASMs will be used for propping during the first two weeks of rehearsals

CC03   Deputy Stage Manager – £375 (TMA Rehearsal Rate) × 4 (Rehearsal Weeks)

CC04   Company Stage Manager – £450 (TMA Rehearsal Rate) × 4 (Rehearsal Weeks)
During the four weeks of rehearsal the CSM will supervise propping and ASMs learning the show. The theatre we will be going to will provide a Stage Manager and therefore the CSM will manage the large cast and also help to operate the show.

CC05   Director – £402 (TMA Weekly) × 4 (Rehearsal Weeks) + £877.34 (Creative Fee)

CC06   Set/Costume Designer – TMA Freelance Designer, Commercial Theatre

CC07   Lighting Designer – TMA Freelance Designer, Commercial Theatre

CC08   Sound Designer – TMA Freelance Designer, Commercial Theatre

CC09   Composer – Estimated compared to other fees

CC10   Production Manager – Estimated compared to other fees and the importance of the role

CC11   Producer – Estimated compared to other fees and the importance of the role

CC12   Audition Costs – 2 days of auditions, room hire. Adverts for auditions will be free but there would be administrative costs e.g. phones, copying, contracts

CC13   Scripts/Copying

CC14   Rehearsal Rooms – The Lyric Hammersmith Rehearsal Rooms &

	Production Office £800 + vat × 4 rehearsal weeks
CC15	Rehearsal Hires – Est. temporary props and furniture for rehearsals
CC16	Set Construction – Est. Materials + Wages
CC17	Props – Est. buy or make, ASMs to do all the work
CC18	Costumes/Wigs – Est. Material + Wages
CC19	Masks – Est. Material + Wages, because actors will have quick changes they can't use makeup to create the animals they are playing
CC20	Advertising – Est. based on £200 advert in two newspapers every week for the month leading up to the show opening, this would also mean that we would be guaranteed an article and a review from both the major newspapers. TV would be too expensive. Radio will be used once the show had opened during the first week.
CC21	FOH Displays – Printing and design for two large displays for the Front of House of the theatre
CC22	Print – 40,000 leaflets, cull colour on both sides (£600) + Posters (£1200)
CC23	Photographer – Est. fee for taking photos at dress rehearsal and photos given to company on CD rom.
CC24	Opening Night/Entertainment – As this is only a short show for children, I thought it wouldn't be a huge Opening Night. Therefore I have budgeted for a drinks reception before and after the performance for the press and other important people.
CC25	Get In/Get Out – Contingency for extra people to help and misc costs
CC26	Transport – Large car to collect set and props from where they have been made.
RC01	Actors, Normal Minimum – £340 (TMA Minimum, Twice Nightly) × 4 (Performance Weeks)
RC02	Actors, Subsistence – £90 × 4 weeks
RC03	Actors, Weekly Touring – £169 × 4 weeks
RC04	Actors, Contingency – Contingency for Understudy obligations and performances
RC05	ASM, Normal Minimum – £340 (TMA Minimum, Twice Nightly) × 4 (Performance Weeks)
RC06	ASM, Subsistence – £90 × 4 weeks
RC07	ASM, Weekly Touring – £169 × 4 weeks
RC08	DSM, Normal Minimum – £425 × 4 weeks
RC09	DSM, Subsistence – £90 × 4 weeks

RC10	DSM, Weekly Touring – £169 × 4 weeks
RC11	CSM, Normal Minimum – £510 × 4 weeks
RC12	CSM, Subsistence – £90 × 4 weeks
RC13	CSM, Weekly Touring – £169 × 4 weeks
RC14	Author/Adaptation – Royalties £90 per performance
RC15	Lighting Hire – Est. The theatre has a lot of lighting and therefore only a small amount in the budget to cover specials
RC16	Sound Hire – Est. Contingency as the theatre has basic sound equipment
RC17	Misc Hire – Contingency
RC18	Repairs – Budget for making repairs to props, set and technical equipment
RC19	Print – Contingency for if posters and leaflets need re-printing
I01	Ticket Sales – Estimated income from ticket sales per week. Calculated as follows: Adult tickets £10, Children £6. Average ticket price £8. The Palace Theatre has 1200 seats, however I have been there to see a similar show and it wasn't full. Therefore I will budget on the assumption that we may only sell 60% of the seats. £8 × 720 (60% of 1200) = £5760 per performance, we plan to do 2 early performance 6 days a week as it is the summer and the show is for children. £5760 × 12 performances = £69,120 per week. However I am relying on a relationship with the theatre that means that they will take 30% of all tickets sales.
I02	Programme Sales – Estimated on selling 200 per performance at £2, with them costing £1 to print × 12 performances. £1 profit × 2400 programmes per week = £2400
I03	Mask Making Workshops – 12 children at a time paying £2 each = £24 income before and after every performance. £576 a week. However it may cost more than this to staff and equip, therefore see I05 (est £1000 costs per week)
I04	Merchandising – Est. sales of books, animal sweets, t-shirts etc...
I05	Local Authority Grant – Would apply for a grant to run the workshops for children. £1000 would mean that we would still make a small profit from the workshops, but would the cheap workshops would also help encourage families to come and see the show.
B01	Capital – Total capital costs
B02	Running – Total running costs
B03	Total of all costs
B04	Total of all costs adding a 15% contingency

B05   Total of all Income

B06   Balance showing estimated profit for the production providing that we sell at least 60% of the seats for every show.

References:

Stage One Website

TMA Website

The Palace Theatre Website

Internet Based Printers Website

The Lyric Hammersmith Website

ASSESSOR FEEDBACK FORM

Assessment Feedback Sheet

The Imaginary High School – Music & Performing Arts Department
National Certificate in Performing Arts

Learner's Name:	Maddy	**Student Number:**	60321

Assignment Title:	Finance budget for regional children's play

Assessor:	Richard Hart	**Assignment Ref:**	03-Budget01

Date Set:	1st February	**Completion Date:**	18th March

Unit Number	Unit Title		Criteria Covered
3	The Performing Arts Business		4

Evidence for assessment complete?	YES		**Is this a Final Assessment?**	YES	

Is this an Interim Assessment?		NO	**Can the student re-submit?**	YES	

Assessment

Unit		Pass			Merit	
3	P4	prepare a production budget for a performing arts event that addresses the essential areas of income and expenditure	✓	M4	prepare a production budget for a performing arts event that addresses most of the relevant areas of income and expenditure with meaningful figures	✓
		Distinction			**Assessor's Comment**	
	D4	prepare a budget for a performing arts event that is comprehensive and accurate based on careful research	✓		This is a very comprehensive and well researched budget and demonstrates a thorough understanding of the production process and this particular performing arts event. The estimated costs are accurate at this stage of approaching investors.	

Assessor's General Comments

Well done, not only have you produced an excellent budget, you have demonstrated that you can think like a producer!

You correctly recognised a need to reduce the cast size for economic reasons and explained how this would work. Like any good producer, I especially liked the fact that you then looked at how the reduction in cast would affect other areas of the production budget. For example, recognising that with quick character changes actors could not use make up to depict the animals and therefore budgeting for masks was an excellent observation.

Deciding to rehearse in London to cut down travel and accommodation costs for your actors was also another example of the many production ideas that you had demonstrating excellent research which enabled you to produce an accurate budget.

Although it is obvious that you have taken ideas from the Stage One website on how to present your budget and explanations, this again demonstrates your use of good research skills to produce a suitable professional document.

Assessor's Name:	Richard Hart		Student's Name:	Maddy
Assessor's Signature:			Student's Signature:	
Date:	21st March		Date:	23rd March

Unit 4: The Historical Context of Performance

Assignment Sheet

The Imaginary High School
Music & Performing Arts Department
National Diploma in Performing Arts (Musical Theatre)

Student Name:		Student Number:	

Assignment Title:	Cabaret in Context

Assessor:	Martin Harris	Assignment Ref:	04-Cabaret01

Date Set:	1st November	Completion Date:	19th December

Unit Number	Unit Title	Criteria Covered
4	The Historical Context of Performance	1, 2, 3

Scenario

You have been asked to research the historical background of the musical *Cabaret* and consider a modern interpretation of the musical by watching the current West End production – presenting your findings to the class on the 19th December.

Grading Criteria

UNIT		Pass		Merit		Distinction
4	P1	describe the background context of an example of performance material, providing some research findings	M1	explain the background context of an example of performance material, providing detailed research findings	D1	provide a comprehensive account of the background context of an example of performance material, providing detailed research findings
4	P2	describe how performance material is contextualised for contemporary use	M2	explain how performance material is contextualised for contemporary use	D2	comprehensively explain how performance material is contextualised for contemporary use
4	P3	communicate the results of research using some presentation skills	M3	communicate the results of research using a range of appropriate presentation skills	D3	communicate the results of research using a range of appropriate presentation skills that effectively communicate all aspects of the researched topics

Task		Action	Criteria	Completed
1.	Research the historical context of the musical *Cabaret*	• Research the background to the creation of the musical *Cabaret*, considering the following influences on the original production: Historical, Social, Political, Economic, Technical, Cultural • Compile a PowerPoint presentation of your research for Interim Assessment	Unit 4 P1, M1, D1	
2.	Present PowerPoint of Historical Context for Interim Assessment **15th November @ 1pm**	Print off your PowerPoint presentation for the historical context of the musical and hand in to the Performing Arts Administration Office by 1.00pm on 15th November	Unit 4 P1, M1, D1	
3.	Research Bill Kenwright's current West End production of *Cabaret*	Watch the current contemporary version of the musical considering its relationship with the original, director's and the creative team's concept, venue, technology, design, current conventions	Unit 4 P2, M2, D2	
4.	Prepare research findings for presentation	Structure your research findings from watching the live show to complete a PowerPoint presentation that could include other presentation materials of your choice.	Unit 4 P3, M3, D3	
5.	Present to the class 19th December	• Present your findings to the class using appropriate presentation equipment: e.g. PowerPoint, audio/video, websites... • Supply a list of resources used during your research.	Unit 4 P1, M1, D1 P2, M2, D2 P3, M3, D3	

N.B. This assignment does not complete the assessment of this unit or the individual criteria targeted within this assignment. Students will have to successfully complete at least another two assignments during the course to meet the requirements of the unit.

Cabaret in Context

By Mike

Cabaret

Cabaret is a musical written in 1966. The story is based on books by Christopher Isherwood who lived in Berlin during the 1930s. In the musical Christopher's name is changed to Clifford Bradshaw and is American.

Cabaret – Broadway Production

- Book – Joe Masteroff
- Lyrics – Fred Ebb
- Music – John Kander
- Producer/Director – Hal Prince
- The musical was going to be called 'Welcome to Berlin'

The Story – Cabaret

The musical of Cabaret has been hugely influenced by the social and cultural conditions of 1930 Berlin.
Germany had lots of problems at the time and it was just before Hitler came to power, all of this can be seen in the show.

Social/Cultural Conditions

- Germany didn't have very much money in 1930s this influenced the song 'Sitting Pretty'. Also the lead actress Sally Bowles is always goes on about money and wanting more.
- The Nazis didn't like Jewish people and the Cabaret story includes two older characters that fall in love and want to get married, but later can't because Herr Schultz is Jewish.

Social/Cultural Conditions

- There is a very funny song called 'If you could see her through my eyes' which has a Gorilla dancing around the stage with the MC. But its not meant to be funny as it is about Jewish people.
- Clifford gets beaten up by Nazis in Act 2, because he has a fight with Ernst who is a Nazis.

Production influences

- The music has only a small band of musicians that play quite badly and out of tune, this depicts the run down club of the time with little money

Production influences

- The cabaret style music is influenced by the composer Kurt Weill.
- Kurt Weill's wife is actually in the Broadway production.
- The staging was influenced by Bertholt Brecht.
- The staging and lighting of the Kit Kat Klub is meant to be really dark and dingy

ASSESSOR FEEDBACK FORM

Assessment Feedback Sheet

The Imaginary High School – Music & Performing Arts Department
National Diploma in Performing Arts (Musical Theatre)

Learner's Name:	Mike	Student Number:	70132

Assignment Title:	Cabaret in Context

Assessor:	Martin Harris	Assignment Ref:	04-Cabaret01

Date Set:	1st November	Completion Date:	15th November

Unit Number	Unit Title	Criteria Covered
4	The Historical Context of Performance	1

Evidence for assessment complete?	YES		Is this a Final Assessment?		NO

Is this an Interim Assessment?	YES		Can the student re-submit?	YES	

Assessment						
Unit	**Pass**			**Merit**		
4	**P1**	describe the background context of an example of performance material, providing some research findings	✓	**M1**	explain the background context of an example of performance material, providing detailed research findings	
	Distinction			**Assessor's Comment**		
	D1	provide a comprehensive account of the background context of an example of performance material, providing detailed research findings		You have made a good attempt to describe the background to the musical *Cabaret*, with some evidence of research that is accurate. However, there was little explanation and detail within this presentation to achieve a better grade. You had lots of interesting statements about the show and its background but you gave little explanation to why, backed up with examples from the show.		

Assessor's General Comments

Your presentation was constructed in a logical way, clearly outlining the historical context of *Cabaret*. Some of the slides would have benefited from being broken up to smaller bullet points, with some being a little too chatty in the way they are written. A relaxed and casual verbal presentation to accompany the PowerPoint can work really well but the slides projected need to use a more professional approach.

To ensure you improve your grades for final assessment, make sure that every statement is clearly backed up with an explanation of why. For example:

Germany didn't have very much money in 1930s this influenced the song 'Sitting Pretty'.

This statement is fine, but you really needed to explore with your research why Germany was in financial trouble, so that you could then have explained how this affected everyone living in Germany and Berlin, and why the song was being sung in the Kit-Kat club as entertainment. If you write further clarification for all your statements your should improve to meet Merit criteria.

Assessor's Name:	Martin Harris		**Student's Name:**	Mike
Assessor's Signature:			**Student's Signature:**	
Date:	18th November		**Date:**	21st November

MERIT LEVEL ANSWER

Cabaret in Context

Research project

Cabaret the musical

Melanie

Cabaret – the musical

Cabaret opened in 1966 produced and directed by Hal Prince, book by Joe Masteroff, lyrics by Fred Ebb, Music by John Kander and Choreography by Ron Field

Cabaret the musical

- In 1930s English writer Christopher Isherwood was living in Berlin, Germany.
- When he left Germany before the war he wrote lots of Novels, one of which included a character called Sally Bowles, an English cabaret singer

Cabaret the musical

- These novels and the character of Sally Bowles inspired John Van Duten to adapt Isherwood's stories into a stage play called 'I am a camera'.
- The play was semi-biographical with a character being like Christopher Isherwood in the story who is an English writer in Berlin who has a relationship with a girl called Sally Bowles

Cabaret the musical

- 'I am a camera' was then changed into a musical by Hal Prince, adding songs by Kander and Ebb.
- The music and style of the production was heavily influenced by the theatre, music and cabaret of Berlin in the 1930s.

 Historical influences

- Money is mentioned quite a lot throughout the show, this is because German people were broke and the country had high un-employment. The song 'Sitting Pretty' and the early conversation between Clifford Bradshaw and Fraulein Schneider show this.
- Germany had huge debts from World War 1 and had to pay lots of money to other countries. Inflation was also out of control and the current government kept printing money to the point of it not being worth much.

 Historical influences

- We all now know about the Nazis wishing to cleanse Germany of other religions and races. The difficulty for Jewish people in Berlin just before Hitler came to power has influenced Cabaret by the story of Herr Schultz who wants to marry Fraulien Schneider, but she ends up turning him down as she is intimidated by the Nazis as Schultz is Jewish.

 Historical influences

- The threat of the Nazis steadily increases throughout the show with their ever growing presence on stage, culminating in the lead actor Clifford Bradshaw getting beaten up by two Nazis because he wouldn't agree with them.
- At the start of the show everyone seems the same, and it very slowly turns out that some people are Nazis and then start appearing with arm-bands on with the Nazis log on them

Historical influences

- The music is heavily influenced by Kurt Weill, which you can hear if you compare the music with some of his shows from 1920s and 30s Germany.
- The staging also resembled that of Brecht and Weill's left-wing theatre productions of the same period, demonstrating avantgarde Berlin theatre.

Historical influences

- Brecht's theatre is very different to standard theatre. He likes to challenge the audience rather than the show being pure entertainment and it is usually very dark and politically driven.
- Both Brecht & Weill had to escape Germany when Hitler came to power as they would have been in danger, because the Nazis didn't like their work. Many of their previous productions were very critical of the Nazis politics

Historical influences

- The sleazy side and sexual freedom of Berlin is demonstrated throughout by the costumes at the Kit-Kat club, the Emcee and songs such as 'Two Ladies' and 'Don't Tell Mama'
- The West Production cast a young actress Dame Judy Dench as Sally Bowles. This might have been because Sally Bowles shouldn't actually be a very good singer. If she was then why would she be stuck working at the Kit-Kat club in Berlin rather than the West End?

ASSESSOR FEEDBACK FORM

Assessment Feedback Sheet

The Imaginary High School – Music & Performing Arts Department

National Diploma in Performing Arts (Musical Theatre)

Learner's Name:	Melanie	Student Number:	70148

Assignment Title:	Cabaret in Context

Assessor:	Martin Harris	Assignment Ref:	04-Cabaret01

Date Set:	1st November	Completion Date:	15th November

Unit Number	Unit Title	Criteria Covered
4	The Historical Context of Performance	1

Evidence for assessment complete?	YES		Is this a Final Assessment?		NO

Is this an Interim Assessment?	YES		Can the student re-submit?	YES	

Assessment					
Unit		Pass		Merit	
4	P1	describe the background context of an example of performance material, providing some research findings	✓	M1 explain the background context of an example of performance material, providing detailed research findings	✓
		Distinction		Assessor's Comment	
	D1	provide a comprehensive account of the background context of an example of performance material, providing detailed research findings		A well structured presentation that goes some way to explain the background to the musical *Cabaret*. Although your research is detailed and covers many of the important points for this show it is not comprehensive, with some statements not clearly accounting for the creative development of the show and the historic influences on it.	

Assessor's General Comments

An example of where you can improve your presentation to meet the Distinction criterion is in the third slide:

When he (Christopher Isherwood) left Germany before the war he wrote lots of Novels...

Although you are absolutely right with this statement it requires a more detailed and comprehensive explanation to answer all the questions that as a reader I am asking myself. Why did he leave Germany? When did he leave? What are the novels? At least one of these questions is quite important.

Another example:

The threat of the Nazis steadily increases throughout the show with their ever growing presence on stage, culminating in the lead actor Clifford Bradshaw getting beaten up by two Nazis because he wouldn't agree with them.

Again you are correct to write this, but you offer little background research to explain why Nazis were increasing in numbers, why their presence within the show becomes more obvious, and your reason for Clifford getting beaten up is far too simplistic and does not reflect the true reasons – his argument with Ernst because he refused to smuggle any more money from Paris to support the Nazis' party propaganda campaigns.

You did quite rightly make some important points about Brecht and Weill's style of theatre; however, to improve your grade, you will also need to consider their influence on the way the songs are used throughout the musical, especially within the context of the Kit-Kat club.

Assessor's Name:	Martin Harris	Student's Name:	Melanie
Assessor's Signature:		Student's Signature:	
Date:	18th November	Date:	21st November

133

Cabaret in Context

Historical Context Research

By Kim

 Cabaret – the musical

- Opened on Broadway in 1966
- West End production opened in 1968
- Made into a film in 1972 starring Liza Minelli

 Cabaret – the musical

- The book and score was originally going to be written by Sandy Wilson, however the producer's option on the novel and play expired…
- Producer & Director Hal Prince picked up the story and commissioned:
  - Joe Masteroff (book)
  - Kander (music) & Ebb (lyrics)
  - Bob Fosse (director/choreographer)

 Cabaret – the musical

- The musical was originally entitled '*Welcome to Berlin*'
- Based on John Van Druten's play '*I Am A Camera*' (1951), the story was semibiographical about a young English writer and his relationship with and English girl Sally Bowles
- This Broadway play was based on Christopher Isherwood's stories of Berlin early 1930s

●●● Isherwood's story...

- In 1930, 26 year-old Englishman – Christopher Isherwood, abandoning medical school, went to Germany to teach English
- He had already tried to write novels and in Berlin, in the last few years of post-war Weimar Republic he found plenty to write about
- A period just before Hitler came to power (Jan 1933) inspired several novels:
  - Mr Morris Changes Train
  - Goodbye To Berlin
  - And the infamous character Sally Bowles

●●● Isherwood's story...

- Isherwood moved to the USA, eventually working for MGM as a scriptwriter and gaining citizenship in 1946
- A prolific writer, nothing became more famous than his work about Berlin in the 1930s

  To understand Cabaret's Historical Context we need to consider the Germany in the 1930s, in particular Berlin!

●●● The Weimar Republic

- 1918 – 1933
- Developed out of defeat and social revolution
- A collective of many different political parties
- Beset by many problems and issues
- Many Germans withheld their support

●●● The Weimar Republic

- After Germany's defeat in World War 1, a national assembly was set up to create a new constitution for the German empire – The Weimar Republic, named after the city of Weimar where the national assembly was set up.
- This period of government had a series of problems to manage...

The Weimar Republic

- Weak Economy
- High rates of inflation
- Unemployment
- Debts from World War 1
- Most pensions & savings wiped out
- History of hung government
- Occupation of parts of Germany by other countries, because of defaults in payments
- Government kept on printing money – so it wasn't worth anything, devaluation.

 ## The Stresemann Era

- A period of the Weimar Republic which produced political stability
- Stresemann survived many coup attempts, including one by Adolf Hitler
- Stresemann negotiated reduced debt payments with other countries
- Unfortunately Stresemann died in 1929

 ## The Third Reich – Hitler

- Adolf Hitler served in World War 1
- He joined the Bavarian German Workers' Party in 1919
- This later became the National Socialist German Workers' Party
- Members were known as Nazis
- Hitler assumed leadership in 1921
- He gathered
  - Un-employed
  - Ex-soldiers
  - Lower middle class
  - Small farmers

The Third Reich – Hitler

- After Hitler's coup failed he was subsequently imprisoned
- He served less than 1 year of a 5 year sentence
- During his year in prison he wrote Mein Kampf (My Struggle)
- This book set out his long-term political terms

●●● The Third Reich & Germany

- Mid 1920s Nazis started with propaganda and legitimising the party
- The great depression (started by Wall Street crash) hit Germany hard
- Loans from US were recalled, bankrupting the country
- Germany was on the verge of civil war

●●● Why Cabaret, Why Hitler?

- The majority of German people were penniless and unemployed, they needed something to get them through their difficult lives. This show highlights two
- The Kit-Kat Club – Cabaret clubs such as the one in the musical Cabaret gave German people a place to go and as the Emcee says in his introduction 'forget all your troubles'
- Through propaganda and intimidation – The Nazi party offered hope to many German people of better times and rebuilding their national pride. This Spring boarded Hitler to government.

●●● Examples of influences...

- **Financial Issues of Germany** – Ernst Ludwig's innocent smuggling turns out to be politically based, to help fund the Nazis party
- **Religion/Race Tentions** – At Fraulien Schneider and Herr Schultz engagement party at the end of Act 1, Schultz sings *Meeskite* an innocent Jewish song. Which divides the guests, Ernst warns Schneider against the marriage and the majority of the guest sing 'Tomorrow Belongs To Me' the show's Nazis anthem.

●●● Historical influences...

- **Political Satire (Kit-Kat Club)** – At the start of Act 2 (Entracte) the big dance number in the Kit-Kat club ends with them dressed as Nazis and doing the goose step.
- **Censorship** – Cliff refuses to go to Paris and smuggle money into the country again for Ernst and tells him what he thinks of the new Nazis politics, he ends up hitting Ernst. Two Nazis then drag him into the streets and beats him up unconscious.
- **Biographical** – The show ends with Cliff starting to write his book as he leaves Berlin.

Cabaret, German, Brecht!

Wonderfully evocative of the Brecht/Weill songs of decadent 1930s Germany, Kander and Ebb's brilliant, sometimes erotic, sometimes deeply frightening score summons up the period with pinpoint accuracy.

 ## Bertholt Brecht (1898–1956)

- Bertholt Brecht was an influential and prolific German socialist, dramatist, stage director and poet in Germany.
- When the Nazis came to power in 1933 he had to go into exile, firstly move to Denmark and then later Sweden and Finland.
- His particular style of theatre, with a strong political drive is still a huge influence on directors today.

 ## Bertholt Brecht (1898–1956)

- Brecht was born into a world of conflict and contradictions.
- By the time he was 16 the First World War had broken out, which consumed Germany with its ferocity and accounted for the deaths of a number of those with whom he went to school.
- Financial, political and personal instability were a way of life and would remain so for Brecht until his death
- He is best known for his 'Epic Theatre' style

 ## Dramatic & Epic Theatre

Dramatic (Standard Director's approach)
- Plot has beginning, middle and end
- Suggests that the spectator is watching real life
- Spectator is involved in something
- One scene makes another to make sense
- Growth – events follow each other in a smooth progression
- Feeling – a theatre where the audience can allow itself to indulge in emotions
- Linear development

●●○ Dramatic & Epic Theatre

Epic Theatre (Brecht's approach)
- Narrative begins anywhere, continues then stops. Issues are not resolved
- Turns the spectator into an observer, but suggests that the spectator can question what she or he is saying
- Forces the audience to take decisions
- Each scene is for itself
- Montage: events are shown in self-contained scenes
- Theatre where the audience is made to question and think

●●○ Brecht's Influences

- Heavily influenced by the funfairs of his youth
- Street entertainment
- Political cabaret
- He was able to draw all these together to make a totally new form of theatre
- The musical Cabaret has all these elements!

●●○ Brecht's Epic Theatre

- Brecht's most important theme in his work was his passionate belief that theatre should not only reflect the world but, more importantly, change it
- He used his theories of Epic Theatre to achieve this in direct contradiction to the prevailing genre of naturalism
- Through this active involvement of the audience, Brecht hoped to draw his audience into the debates within the texts, which were based on moral and political dilemmas within the Communist arena

●●○ Brecht & Kurt Weill

- Kurt Weill worked with Brecht very closely on many productions as a composer.
- Their masterpiece Rise and Fall of the City of Mahagonny, caused an uproar when it premiered in 1930 in Leipzig, with Nazis in the audience protesting. When it later premiered in a then, more liberal Berlin in 1931, it was a triumphant sensation.
- Songs tended to comment on the action to reinforce and amplify the text's meaning, rather than move the actual story on.
- Both Brecht and Weill eventually moved to America to escape the threat of the Nazis

Brecht's influences...

- The stage musical is like 2 musicals in 1:
  - The first being a traditional musical format where a song will come out of dialogue and either comment on what the character is feeling or move the story on. For example: early in Act 1 the song *So What* sung by Fraulein Schneider comes out of haggling over the rent for one of her rooms with Clifford Bradshaw. Although there is nothing natural about suddenly an orchestra striking up and dialogue turning into song, these scenes are played for real. They are naturalistic in approach.

 Brecht's influences...

- The second is the Brecht/Weill influence of songs used within the Kit-Kat club as cabaret songs. On the surface they are silly songs for entertainment, but the meanings run much deeper. Here are some examples...

 Brecht's influences...

- The song *Two Ladies* early in Act 1, is a silly song about regularly sleeping with two women. However it helps to set a real feel of the seedy Berlin of 1930s, especially as the Emcee singing the song is far from being a typical straight guy.
- The song *Sitting Pretty* is back in the Kit-Kat club, where the Emcee is singing about everyone needing money, but 'I have all the money I need'. Again relevant for the audience of 1930 Germany, but the song has also just followed a scene where we have found out that Ernst's smuggling is to fund the Nazis party.

 Brecht's influences...

- *If You Could See Her Through My Eyes* a song that through out seems entirely innocent, where the Emcee sings of no one understanding his love for a Gorilla dressed as a girl and that dances with him. It is a lovely song that could be seen as being entirely politically correct and a lesson to us all about tolerance of others, until the sting in the tail – the last line of the song...

'She wouldn't look Jewish at all'

●●○ Brecht's influences...

- In the Nazis propaganda of the time Jewish people would be depicted in cartoons as Gorillas among other things. The song for modern day audiences can have a huge effect, as you are listening away innocently laughing to the song, the sudden realisation and possible guilt to the contemporary audience of laughing at what is a very sick joke really drives Brecht's dramatic approach of making his audience think about what they are watching, shocking where necessary.
- This song is also sandwiched perfectly between a brick being thrown through Schultz (Jewish) shop window and Schneider returning Sally and Cliff's engagement present and telling them that the wedding is off.

●●○ Brecht's influences...

- Even Sally Bowle's infamous return to the Kit-Kat club at the end of Act 2 to sing the classic feel-good song Cabaret has a poignant ring to it as it takes over from the sounds of Cliff being beaten up outside the club by Nazis.

'Live is a cabaret old chum...'

●●○ Brecht's influences...

- Interestingly when the musical was first written it was intended to be a play followed by songs describing 1930s Berlin, but it soon took on the structure of a more traditional musical with the songs dispersed between and evolving from dialogue scenes.
- In the later film version only the songs within the Kit-Kat club survived, making the film much more gritty and even more Brecht like in the use of cabaret style songs.

●●○ Production influences...

- The original Broadway cast featured Lotte Lenya as Fraulein Schneider. Lotte was Kurt Weil's wife.
- The character of Christopher Isherwood in the musical became Clifford Bradshaw who was American not English. Probably to please Broadway audiences.
  - In the film version as they wanted Liza Minelli to play Sally, (therefore Sally had to be American), they turned Cliff into Brian and back to English.

ASSESSOR FEEDBACK FORM

Assessment Feedback Sheet

The Imaginary High School – Music & Performing Arts Department
National Diploma in Performing Arts (Musical Theatre)

Learner's Name:	Kim	Student Number:	70136

Assignment Title:	Cabaret in Context

Assessor:	Martin Harris	Assignment Ref:	04-Cabaret01

Date Set:	1st November	Completion Date:	15th November

Unit Number	Unit Title	Criteria Covered
4	The Historical Context of Performance	1

Evidence for assessment complete?	YES		Is this a Final Assessment?		NO

Is this an Interim Assessment?	YES		Can the student re-submit?	YES	

Assessment				
Unit		Pass		Merit
4	**P1** describe the background context of an example of performance material, providing some research findings	✓	**M1** explain the background context of an example of performance material, providing detailed research findings	✓
	Distinction		**Assessor's Comment**	
	D1 provide a comprehensive account of the background context of an example of performance material, providing detailed research findings	✓	This is excellent work and is very comprehensive in outlining your research to the historical background of the musical *Cabaret*. Your research findings are clear and detailed. Well Done!	

Assessor's General Comments

A lot of background research is evident within the PowerPoint that has resulted in some of the slides being rather cramped. It would be a good idea for the final presentation, to thin out some of the slides and use the research within your notes for the verbal explanation. PowerPoint is much better when it displays snappy short bullet points, if you have very long sentences on the projector your audience will tend to read it rather than listen to you.

Make sure you double-check your research when you are writing it up to ensure that you haven't made a mistake. As you also briefly considered the film version you have confused who did the choreography for the theatre show. For the original Broadway production, Ron Field choreographed; Bob Fosse choreographed and directed the later film version in 1972. However, this is a common mistake for people to make.

Assessor's Name:	Martin Harris	Student's Name:	Kim
Assessor's Signature:		Student's Signature:	
Date:	18th November	Date:	21st November

Unit 20: Applying Acting Styles

Assignment Sheet

The Imaginary High School
Music & Performing Arts Department
National Award in Performing Arts (Acting)

Student Name:		Student Number:	

Assignment Title:	Monologues & Duologues

Assessor:	Kay Pringle	Assignment Ref:	20-MonDuo01

Date Set:	19th October	Completion Date:	7th December

Unit Number	Unit Title	Criteria Covered
20	Applying Acting Styles	1, 2, 3, 4

Scenario

During your Acting classes, you will have participated in practical exercises focusing on characterisation, preparing and observing characters using Stanislavski techniques. Decisions as to the interpretation of the duologues and monologues, the characterisation and the possible staging, will be explored and developed during the rehearsal process, and you are expected to show imagination and initiative in this aspect of the assignment. This assignment requires you to perform in one monologue and one duologue in the Drama Studio at the end of term.

Grading Criteria

UNIT		Pass		Merit		Distinction
20	P1	research a character, drawing simple conclusions about the nature of the role	M1	research a character, accounting for the creative process in developing a role	D1	research a character, giving a comprehensive and reasoned account of the creative process and fully supporting their conclusions about the role
20	P2	develop rudimentary skills and techniques for the realisation of a character/role, demonstrating some grasp of the specific demands upon the actor of particular texts, in relation to the style of acting	M2	develop sound skills and techniques for the realisation of character/role, demonstrating a sound grasp of the specific demands upon the actor of particular texts, in relation to the style of acting	D2	develop advanced skills and techniques for the realisation of a character/role, demonstrating a comprehensive grasp of the specific demands upon the actor of particular texts, in relation to the style of acting
20	P3	develop material for performance through rehearsal, with support and guidance	M3	develop material for performance through rehearsal, with minimum support and guidance	D3	independently develop material for performance through rehearsal

Grading Criteria							
UNIT		Pass		Merit		Distinction	
20	P4	interpret and realise a text, showing some understanding of the material and its performance demands and communicating some ideas and feelings to an audience	M4	interpret and realise a text, showing sound understanding of the material and its performance demands, communicating effectively with an audience	D4	interpret and realise a text, showing thorough understanding of the material and its performance demands, communicating ideas and feelings with concentration and commitment	

Task		Action	Criteria	Completed
1.	Select a monologue and a duologue	• You will participate in read-throughs and discussions of a variety of contemporary plays and choose a monologue and a duologue • You will provide an account of research into character which you will record in your logbook	Unit 20 P1, M1. D1	
2.	Building characters using Stanislavski's system	You will develop both of your characters with imagination and interpretation of clues contained within the text using Stanislavski's system of developing characters. You will reflect on the rehearsal period in your logbook.	Unit 20 P1, M1, D1 P2, M2, D2	
3.	Monologue and duologue rehearsals	• You will interpret your text showing thorough understanding of your material and its performance demands which you will record in your logbook. • You will clearly communicate your character's intentions, feelings and attitude to the audience.	Unit 20 P3, M3, D3	
4.	Written evidence to be handed in to the Performing Arts Administration Office **6th December by 3.30pm**	Please hand your written work in after morning dress rehearsal, this should include: • Logbooks for each week • Character Analysis for both pieces	Unit 20 P1, M1, D1	
5.	Perform pieces in Drama Studio **7th December @ 2pm**	Your performance will be consistent, focused and accurate in use of physical and vocal expression to convey character, mood, intention and feeling.	Unit 20 P4, M4, D4	

N.B. This assignment does not complete the assessment of this unit or the individual criteria targeted within this assignment. Students will have to successfully complete at least another two assignments during the course to meet the requirements of the unit.

UNIT 20: APPLYING ACTING STYLES
GRAHAM

Acting Log

WEEK 1

Tasks:
- Warm-ups
- Assignment explained
- Researching suitable Monologues and Duologues

I was pleased with how work went this week. I think that the approach we took has helped us look at a range of different ideas and then we have been able to make a good decision on which one we should choose. I am pleased with the scene I have chosen to do, I think that it is an interesting and unusual concept and whilst the situation of stalking and being stalked as well as the idea of psychological murder induced by love is one that has been hit on before I think that seeing someone in this very disturbed sort of mind set confessing his love and how obsessive he is to the person who he has these feelings for is not something I think often found within theatre.

I think that my character in the duologue needs to sound very odd and obviously at a very poignant moment in his life, I want to give the slight feel that the speech he gives is rehearsed and he had gone over it and over it in his mind many time before this day comes. I think that that feeling of precise knowing of what is going on at all times and a knowing of exactly what he is going to say next is a very creepy thing to add to a character's persona. I want my character to be as dramatically effective as possible, so I will need to put in a lot of time on working on the character, I think 'hot seating' will be a very valuable technique for me to use at some stage in creating this character as to start thinking like him, answering questions like him and behaving like he would be around other people, will really help me in finding the character's mannerisms.

I am pleased with how this week's session has gone. I think that it has been very productive; I think that if we get off to a good start next week in creating our characters more fully and working on the whole scene then we will be on track to create a strong piece.

WEEK 2

- Warm up
- Continued work on our 'Confessions' piece
- Looking at Stanislavski influenced questions on our characters

Again I am pleased with what we have achieved this session, I think that we worked well and made good progress with our piece. We really tried to get our work off of the page this week and to get up and moving with it. We started to block it and look at the scenes around our two confessions in more detail. Which not only obviously helps to create the piece as a whole but did help me to work on my confession as it gave it more of a context, which helped to make it more real I felt.

I found the Stanislavski questions on my character a little challenging but very helpful. I found them tricky as he is such an odd and extreme character and within this scene he very much has two faces. Even things such as his age I found very interesting to think about. As I think he isn't actually very old, but has the air of an older person about him, because of his intelligence and the precision, which he must possess to carry out the life that he does. I think after using the Stanislavski questions I do have a better understanding of who my character really is, as well as, which for this character is more important that ever; who he wants people to believe him to be.

Overall I think that this week has been very successful in many ways. I think that we have made progress on the scene in many different ways; including simply blocking it but also working on character and the dialogue. So I am pleased and although we still have a little way to go. I think that we are on track to create a good piece.

WEEK 3

• Warm up
• Continued work on our 'Confessions' piece

I feel we made less progress this week on our piece than we have over the last two weeks but this is probably a sign that we are nearer to getting to where we want to get and therefore there is less that needs changing all the time. I think we have made all the necessary changes we needed to make to the script now and I think that we simply need to tighten up the piece with rehearsal.

This week I found getting into the character for rehearsing more difficult. I have put this mainly down to the fact that we were stuck in a small room with all the other groups as no other space was really available for us to use.

I think that the work we did on the physical aspects of our performance was very valuable however. We had decided that we wanted there to be a fight or struggle of some kind but we had not yet worked this out. This week we looked at choreographing the struggle to make it look real and dramatically interesting, I think we succeeded in creating a realistic fight that gives the audience the right feel. The rehearsal of the piece continued and the performance got tighter generally. I think that as the piece is set in a confined space (a lift) that it is important that we decide on a size of space that we can use and then stick to it for all rehearsals. This will make the performance easier as we will be more used to using the certain space, which will be particularly important for the more physical side of the performance.

During rehearsals this week I experimented with a stutter for my character before the transition into the maniac. I think that this stutter will make the transition more unexpected and therefore have more of an impact on the audience.

Although we maybe did not make as much progress as we have done over past weeks I think that we have built the piece up more and we are still on track to create a good scene by the end of the rehearsal process.

WEEK 4

• Warm up

- Continued work on our 'Confessions' piece

I think that this week was fairly productive; I think that rehearsals for the piece went well and that now we are at the stage of putting the finishing touches to it and making sure we are happy with it. We made a couple of minor alterations to the piece this week and ran through it a few times to put some polish on it.

I think we are ready for next week to perform the piece. I was a little concerned however as I thought we would not have run through it in nearly a week but we will be getting some extra time to rehearse the piece in the morning before the assessment and even a little time the day before which I am pleased about. The one problem is that so far we have not rehearsed with props yet. This shouldn't cause too much of a problem though, as the props are quite minimal. So as long as we remember them it will be fine.

I am pleased with the runs of the piece that we have done today. As I have mentioned I think that the skeleton of the piece is now firmly in place and it is just a question of running it as much as we can to ensure we know it, double check for any issues, to make ourselves more confident about it and to generally tighten the piece up.

Overall I think that I feel more confident about the piece now than I did a week ago and even then I though I would at this stage last week. Therefore I am pleased and I think with a little more rehearsal; the opportunity for which we have next week, we will have a strong piece which we can be proud of.

WEEK 5

- Final rehearsals of our piece
- Performance of our duologue and my monologue

Overall I am pleased with our performance; I think that the assessed performance was the best that we have ever done it. I think that in particular the movement in the piece around the space when my character starts to peruse and tries to corner the character that he is obsessed with was strong during the assessed performance.

I was pleased with my performance to an extent I think that the false stutter that I put in worked well and really added a nice layer to piece. However when the character shows his true colours as a very dangerous man with a very serious obsession with the other character in the piece I think my character was a little weak. I think that I needed to make him more frightening and alarming for the other character. I think that the other character was a hard one to play naturalistically, so that the audience really believed her. I think that possibly I did not give her enough to react to, in an emotional and vocal sense, making her part a little harder to play. While I think that the movement between both characters was strong, particularly in the final performance.

I think the developing relationship in the scene was also quite well represented. I think that it was believable that these two people had just met, but at the same time it was believable during the character change that my character had been watching her for a long time and knew much about her life.

In conclusion I think that the piece went really well and we achieved everything that we wanted to within it. As I have said I think, and I am please that the assessment performance was the best performance of the piece we have ever done.

'Confessions' – Male Character

How old am I:
30

What is my class?
I am middle class, I have enough money however not to have to work. I live in a comfortable house and have no trouble in providing for myself.

What is by breeding?
I am from a middle class background as well. I was brought up well by my mother, my father I never knew. I however left home at a young age due to a falling out with my mother, fuelled by my antisocial behaviour as a younger man.

What am I like physically?
Quite tall, tall enough to be intimidating. Very still at times. I have slightly slumped shoulders. There is nothing particularly disturbing about my physical appearance except for my stillness and possibly also the fact that I stare quite a lot.

What am I like mentally?
Very obsessive and mentally disturbed. Very intelligent, but use my intellect for bad rather than for good or productive things. I have an obsession with the other character in the piece; Lucy who I have been following for over two years. This obsession has been leading up to the meeting, which takes place in the piece.

What are my strengths?
Intelligence and being able to hide my obsessions and evil calculating nature from everyone. I am able to act and behave normally all the time if required.

What are my weaknesses?
My obsessions that I have are the lack of self-control and insanity that I have when it come to the objects of my desire. The need to own people.

What do others think of me?
Nobody knows of my obsessions, so I believe that most people believe my facade. I am a fairly good judge of people's character because I have an intelligent and realistic mind.

Do I know what they think?
I believe I know that nobody is aware of my true colours but some may not like me for other reasons. However I do not believe there is much that I do not now about the people I interact with due to my good ability to 'work people out'. If I did not understand someone I am enough of a realistic to be able to admit that I didn't understand that person to myself and then I would try to find out more through other means.

What way do I speak?
Quite well spoken and polite when behaving normally very slow and methodical in speech when in a bizarre mindset.

What are my personal patterns-daily routines/hobbies?
Simply watching Lucy the girl that I am obsessed with.

What is my emotional age?
45

ASSESSOR FEEDBACK FORM

Assessment Feedback Sheet

The Imaginary High School – Music & Performing Arts Department
National Award in Performing Arts (Acting)

Learner's Name:	Graham	Student Number:	70068

Assignment Title:	Monologues & Duologues

Assessor:	Kay Pringle	Assignment Ref:	20-MonDuo01

Date Set:	19th October	Completion Date:	7th December

Unit Number	Unit Title	Criteria Covered
20	Applying Acting Styles	1

Evidence for assessment complete?	YES		Is this a Final Assessment?		NO

Is this an Interim Assessment?	YES		Can the student re-submit?	YES	

Assessment

Unit		Pass			Merit	
20	P1	research a character, drawing simple conclusions about the nature of the role	✓	M1	research a character, accounting for the creative process in developing a role	

		Distinction		Assessor's Comment		
	D1	research a character, giving a comprehensive and reasoned account of the creative process and fully supporting their conclusions about the role		You developed a very basic interpretation of your character in your reflective working logbook. You were able to justify some character choices, however these were very limited. You focused mostly on how pleased you felt with the session rather then how you used research and practitioner knowledge to help develop character.		

Assessor's General Comments
Graham, you worked fairly well in this assignment, you demonstrated a fairly good understanding of the characters you played. You demonstrated a reasonably good understanding of Stanislavki's techniques during the lessons; however you struggled to reflect on them in your individual rehearsal process and in your reflective working logbook. You state in your logbook that you think it would be valuable for you to use hot seating as part of your character development, however you never discuss why or even attempt to try and use it. You also state that after answering the Stanislavski questions you have a better idea of what kind of character he is, however you do not give any examples or reflect on how this has assisted you during the rehearsal period. You also tended to focus on one emotion in your questions. You must make sure for future assignments that you justify all of your character choices by ensuring you do lots of relevant research in order to achieve a more three dimensional character.

Assessor's Name:	Kay Pringle
Assessor's Signature:	
Date:	7th December

UNIT 20: APPLYING ACTING STYLES
CLAIRE

Week 1

- Physical warm-up
- Vocal warm-up
- Assignment brief
- Performance on Top Girls Shona
- Looking at subtext on research for mono/duo

Today in my acting lesson we did some physical warm-ups from head to toe. I feel really relaxed when doing exercises in the form of a circle a method to make me aware of people I will be seen to work with. It has been quoted by, Stanislavski that he found by doing exercises such as physical warm-up "the unwanted tension has been eliminated so performers attain a state of physical and vocal relaxation".

I believe this quote because, when I do any of the warm-ups in class I find I am at ease and in a relaxed frame of mind physically and mentally, it helps me in my performances and give me time to experience emotions from my past experiences in playing characters on stage. I feel if we didn't have our physical warm-up at the start of our lesson our performances would be both mechanical and unrealistic in believing in our characters.

Vocal warm-ups ensure that I maintain my character's emotions and ensure good projection which is more than effective on stage. Feeling more in my vocal skills enables me to attain my state of emotions when portraying different characterisations. I feel more relaxed and comfortable when expressing myself vocally when we lead one another in verses. This is to keep everyone at a certain level of energy when reciting different use of alliteration and tongue twisters. Doing this together helps me in a lot of ways to express myself and to others in group work, when improvising and devising for performances.

Today our assignment was set to find a monologue and duologue, while researching the plays and characters.

I feel more panicky than nervous when I am set assignments but reading through the assignment brief and talking through my problems with Kay helped me.

Once I have decided on both my monologue and duologue I will practice with my lines to understand the monologues piece so that it made it easier for me to react, pause at the right time and to help with physicality in my expression in my body and facial expressions of the character

The research I will gather will ensure I get a sense of truth when playing my character but will also thinking about between the lines (subtext), the magic if when expressing the role so that I can make it believable so the audience could respond well to my interpretation of my character.

Having tried it through my monologue I felt my weaknesses was at the start when I had rushed through my lines because I was feeling nervous and my nerves made me deliver my lines more quickly until the end when it became believable as I slowed down the pace, added pronunciation where I felt it was needed. I found as I read Top Girls play, it helped me to understand my character further. It allowed me to see how my character did everything in her power to get the sales position post, enabling her to live the life she's always craved for. To refer to her interview with Nell the interviewer she pretends to be someone that she's not so that she can experience the life she's always wanted. In a society where males were dominating that era in time of Mrs Thatcher's first term of Prime Minister of Britain, this was a particularly hard thing for my character to overcome.

I empathize a lot with Shona; I've experienced times when I've dressed up to make myself look older in front of my sister's friend when they came over. Its natural and its really damaging to our self esteem when you don't get the opportunity to be accepted for who you are.

Week 2

- Physical warm-up
- Vocal warm-up
- Breathing counts
- Working on Mono/duo

I really enjoyed doing the breathing counts. I'm starting to feel improvement in my ability to maintain and control my breathing, which is important to the delivery of my lines, when rehearsing for my monologue and duologue.

My rehearsal stages are starting to come together nicely. I have been memorising my monologue, reflecting on the role of my character to the situation and thinking about how the character is perceived in my duologue. I think to make sure I remember the basic facts of my character when I start the scene. Marlene is forty something and had a good backbone in her career as Manager of Top Girls Employment Agency.

I've looked at the subtext and Stanislavski questions and applied them to my character profile of Jackie. I have thought about the characters situation, objective and emotional expression.

I've carefully inspected my monologues as I have discovered a lot about my character, how she experienced heartache when she had to give away her illegitimate child for the sake of the dominating society she was living in, the fact that she had to watch the child grow into a beautiful teenager, with not knowing that her so called sister is in fact her real mother. It's hard on any mother to leave her child, but since her mother Margaret experienced the same ordeal with Jackie she understood the consequences of her actions and that affected her personally and drove Jackie to let go of something as precious as her own child, she tries to plead to Rosie when Rosie confronts her.

Week 3

- Physical warm-up
- Vocal warm-up
- Relaxation exercises
- Rehearsal for duo and mono

The relaxation exercises help me to prepare for the expression in movement when I can perform my piece to class and by the exercise done in lesson I will outline how to react to the lines spoken remembering to use the units and objective handout and to refer back to Stanislavski questions as it will just guide me to find my character's emotional space and reflect on my emotional space using past experiences and using my imagination.

With the scene I have considered various ways of blocking and how we will present it and stage it in front of the class. I think this will be benefit us of we prepare early for our assessment date.

I need to know the background of my character, delivering lines correctly and expressing the character's emotions effectively. Each play has a historical background I can research on and find the true-life basis of the character. For example: Marlene – this clever able career woman managing director of Top Girl's Employment Agency in relationship to Mrs Thatcher's appointment as Prime Minister.

Set in the early eighties the period when Mrs Thatcher's first term of office as Prime Minister. It addresses a lot of themes through the male dominating society with the roles, expectations and shared experiences of women at the same time.

I must understand the character in order to deliver the lines correctly. I will need to analyse the scene, determine the situation, and decide how this situation affects my character. Using research and own personal experiences I can decide how the character would feel in this situation, and how this event in the play will affect the character. I will express what I think the character would be feeling when saying the lines.

Week 4

- Physical warm-up
- Vocal warm-up
- Breathing counts
- Rehearsal – mono/duo

When Theresa and I performed our piece to the class it was evident to suggest that we didn't have much time rehearsing as Theresa forgot her lines but I think we just need to spend more time working on it together to get it almost perfect ready to perform as part of our assessment.

The rehearsal period is the best way to keep focus and concentrate on the atmosphere that should be built within our characters, that way we can interpret the duologue more naturally when we come to show it to the class.

I enjoy the rehearsal period as it gives me time to reflect on the given circumstances of the character and emotions that my character is going through. It also enables me to work on staging, blocking and to understand the situations that the character faces. It also allows me to see how each line needs to mean something and that I need to understand everything about the characters lives in order to achieve a realistic interpretation of character

Week 5

- Physical warm-up
- Vocal warm-up
- Breathing counts
- Rehearsal – running through monologues

The rehearsal was good for both monologues and duologues. We ran through lines, ensured we both knew the staging and I could feel a lot of improvement with the learning of our lines

My monologue piece is going so well. I have practised it through with family and friends and tried it out with feedback from fellow actors in my class, this has really helped me to express the changes needed in emotional expression and I just need to emphasise more as I have to plead to Rosie to forgive me for keeping the secret that I was her mother from her.

My duologue piece is starting to show good energy levels. If I incorporate my monologue with my duologue I can see a lot of similarities and a lot of differences as well because both characters Jackie and Marlene are older, both had illegitimate children, both chose to keep it from them. The differences were as Marlene is a career woman and felt that her career came first, with Jackie she had no other choice in the matter she didn't want to lose Rosie but, with the persuasion on her mother's experience she didn't know what to do under the circumstances of being rejected in society, being called the black sheep of the family.

Week 6

- Physical warm-up
- Vocal warm-up
- Breathing counts
- Dress rehearsal – running monologues and duologues

The dress rehearsal was good preparation in how we needed it to be presented on the assessment date. There was more structure which helped me feel more confident and relax about performing to the class because, I knew that things were in order and it helps me to remain in focus on other things that were not in order such as my duologue with Theresa.

I think it would help if I had a prop or costume to distinguish my character's role through Top Girls and most importantly in trying to get hold of Theresa so we can do a final run though together with our lines.

My monologue was more of a serious tone to that of my duologue as I plead to my own daughter to forgive me in what I thought was best for her at the time.

My duologue was really an awkward tone as Angie bursts into my office, without knocking, making my feelings abrupt from the start as I answer to her. I try to dodge her questions by asking about Joyce because; I want to know why she's come into my life when things seemed to be going well for her

She treats Angie as if she was a client implying that she is more interested in her career than her own child. Angie comes in unannounced therefore I needed to get to the bottom of things in why is she here and why now?

Monologue on My Mother Said I Never Should by Charlotte Keatley
Scene Rosie confronts Jackie on choosing her life over having a child

Who am I? Jackie – mother to Rosie

Where am I? I am with Rosie at my home (Margaret and Ken)

What do I want? I want Rosie to forgive me and try to make amends and for me to be her mother again

Why do I want it: Because I feel I've missed out so much in her life that I just want to get to know her

Why do I want it now? I'm not going to make the same mistake twice

What will happen if I don't get it? I will breakdown since I lost mum and maybe the only chance with my own daughter

How will I get what I want? I want to explain the past, the time period when I was a kid myself I wasn't able to look after you the way you wanted

What must I overcome? The tension between Rosie and myself. I want to make her understand how much I loved her and still do and want her to believe I only did what I did for her own good.

Where am I going? I am going to the park to confront Rosie

Where am I coming from? I'm coming from mum's place where Rosie confronts me about being her real mum

Who am I talking to? I am pleading to Rosie to forgive me and let me be a part of her life

What is my relationship to them? I'm Rosie's Mother

What do I expect from them? I expect her to forgive me for making the mistake of losing her over my career.

How do I get it? By explaining how it was difficult at the time.

Do I get it? I don't know if she'll ever forgive me and my head is swimming out of control

If not, what happens? I don't know. I will not be able to live with myself

What has happened before? My mother Margaret who raised Rosie has died from cancer.

Duologue on Top Girls by Caryl Churchill

Scene Angie walks into Top Girls Employment Agency to see Marlene

Who am I? Marlene

Where am I? In my office at Top Girls Employment Agency

What do I want? I want to be successful in life knowing how much I've had to struggle

Why do I want it? I want it because I want to prove to idle gossip that I am more capable than any man

Why do I want it now? I feel that it's the right time since I haven't got family that I need to think about

What will happen if I don't get it? I will feel outraged and that will give me more focus

How will I get what I want? I won't let anyone stand in my way especially Angie

Where am I going? I'm going to Joyce's home and taking Angie with me. I can't have her staying with me and finding out I am her mother it would ruin all my hopes and dreams

Where am I coming from? I'm coming from the Top Girl's Agency

Who am I talking to? Talking to Angie about why she's come and if I could try to find a way of getting her to talk, bribe her with outings to lunch, Madam Tussauds and be nice to her

What is my relationship to them? Relationship is supposedly Niece and Aunty but in fact Daughter and Mother

What do I expect from them? I want her to leave me be

How do I get it? By explaining

Do I get it? By confronting her telling her to go and get out of my life

What has happened before? Before, either just getting off the phone to a client or working through the paperwork unaware what was about to happen

ASSESSOR FEEDBACK FORM

Assessment Feedback Sheet

The Imaginary High School – Music & Performing Arts Department
National Award in Performing Arts (Acting)

Learner's Name:	Claire	Student Number:	70068

Assignment Title:	Monologues & Duologues

Assessor:	Kay Pringle	Assignment Ref:	20-MonDuo01

Date Set:	19th October	Completion Date:	7th December

Unit Number	Unit Title	Criteria Covered
20	Applying Acting Styles	1

Evidence for assessment complete?	YES		Is this a Final Assessment?		NO
Is this an Interim Assessment?	YES		Can the student re-submit?	YES	

Assessment					
Unit		Pass		Merit	
20	P1	research a character, drawing simple conclusions about the nature of the role	✓	M1 research a character, accounting for the creative process in developing a role	✓
		Distinction		Assessor's Comment	
	D1	research a character, giving a comprehensive and reasoned account of the creative process and fully supporting their conclusions about the role		You gave a fairly good account of your character development in your logbook; however you did not demonstrate enough understanding of practitioner knowledge in relation to your developing character. You made some references to how you used practitioner knowledge to assist your developing character; however your lack of detailed research prevented you from achieving more then a merit.	

Assessor's General Comments
Claire, you worked well in this assignment. During the lessons you demonstrated a fairly good understanding of Stanislavski's techniques, however you did not reflect on these in enough detail in your working logbook. You clearly reflected on your strengths and weaknesses when discussing your developing character, however your lack of character research prevented you from making confident actor choices. You must make sure that for future assignments you read the plays inside-out and complete all of your practitioner character research exercises so that you can achieve an excellent understanding of the characters you are playing. At times your grammar is a little confusing; you must make sure you check your work before handing it in to ensure correct spellings and sentence structures.

Assessor's Name:	Kay Pringle
Assessor's Signature:	
Date:	7th December

DISTINCTION LEVEL ANSWER

UNIT 20: APPLYING ACTING STYLES
DANIEL

Actors Log

WEEK 1

Activities: Physical and vocal warm up. Exercises to help build character. Introduction to the assignment

We started the session with a discussion of the acting monologue and duologue assignment. I am really looking forward to it as we are able to choose our pieces. I have been reading a range of plays so am hoping I will be able to find something exciting and challenging.

We then looked at some exercises to help build character. We started with a simple observation task, where we had to go and observe someone in the college and make notes on their physicality and behaviour. We were asked to go in to as much detail as possible and were given a check list to fill out. I found this utterly compelling as the person I choose was so loud and brash and appeared to be so confident. I was fortunate enough to have hung around for long enough to see that this was not the case when they were caught drinking in the library. Their whole demeanour changed and they seemed genuinely embarrassed. Their physically changed, retreating back in to their seat not speaking to anyone even when the librarian went away. It made me realise how quickly we judge people and assume they are a certain type of person without thinking about how they are affected in different situations. I am going to make sure that when I start to work on my characters for my assessment that I see the character as three dimensional and not just focus on one aspect of their personality or one emotion that they face.

We reflected on some of the Stanislavski exercises we had done in previous workshops, we discussed how we were going to apply our exercises to our individual character development. We then worked through some emotional memory exercises where we closed our eyes and tried to recall the first time we had experienced the following: first time we heard the waves, the first time we heard the wind rustling through the trees, the first time we listened to a sad song, the smell of a rotten egg and of newly mowed grass. I found that I had a clear reaction to the smell of a rotten egg and the first time I heard the waves. I felt instantly sick when I thought about the egg and found myself getting quite tearful when I thought about the waves. A particular memory stood out for me too. I felt sad and elated at the same time and found it strange and exciting to be able to feel two contrasting emotions from a memory. It made me realise that any character I end up playing can feel a range of emotions with one line, I must be careful not to generalise the piece and focus on the same emotion the whole way though. I need to think about the character's life and make sure I am able to make relevant emotional choices.

WEEK 2

Activities: Physical and vocal warm up. Stanislavski exercises to help build character's lives.

We started the session by discussing how to annotate our texts. We looked at how to break the pieces up in to units and objectives in order to make believable actor choices. We looked at clues on stage directions and our relationships with other characters. We looked at Stanislavski's basic 7 questions and started to fill them in about our characters. I was unsure on which pieces to chose as I had two really good monologues that I felt were challenging and that I would able to do justice with. After speaking with my tutor Kay, she advised me to read both of the plays that the monologues were from and then make the final decision for next session.

We then went and did some research. I ended up researching both plays. I read a synopsis of both plays and found some interesting work on the playwrights. I then tried to decipher the themes and issues of both pieces and why the playwrights wrote them. I also wrote a list of the journey the character goes on and the emotions that character faces during the monologues. I then thought about the given circumstances of the character, what I would do in that situation and how would I feel. I then wrote another list of similarities and differences between me and the character. I found all of these tasks really useful as I was able to understand both characters a lot better. I was also able to focus on what the character is actually trying to say and how it makes them feel. I felt a lot more confident in making the final decision on what piece I was going to do after completing these exercises.

WEEK 3

Activities: Physical and vocal warm up, words in different emotions, scene – using words from a list, work on monologue for assignment.

Going around the class in a circle everyone had to say various words/phrases in a different emotion from what everyone else had said. This exercise proved challenging as I found I would have to change form how I planned to attempt the words if the person just before me did as I was planning. The benefit I found from this was that it meant that I had to think fast and prepare several emotional options for how to say each word/phrase. It was difficult to do a different emotion every time and some of what I did wasn't as believable as I could have been, but under the circumstances of the exercise I don't think what I did went badly.

Using the list of phrases and working with Charlie I had to create a short scene using only the listed words. The scenario we devised saw me trying to convince Charlie not to go somewhere that she was going. To show the emotions in this scene I drew on past experiences that have been similar. Feedback we received suggested alternative ways to approach the scene, which I believe helped the focus of the emotions in the scene.

Working on the Monologues and Duologues assignment this week I had to choose pieces to work on. For my monologues I will be working on a scene from Sweet Panic by Stephen Poliakoff. The copy of the monologue I have came from The Methuen Audition book for Men so I will have to obtain a full copy of the play to fully learn what I can about the role I will be playing. The character I will be playing will be interesting to develop as in the play it is one character doing an impression of another. The audition book states that the part can be played out of context as the character that is being impersonated, which is how I intend to tackle the role. I think that this monologue will be good for me to work on as I like its pace of story telling and I think it'll give me possibility to show varied depth of emotion.

For the duologue I will be working with Doug, although at this time we have been unable to settle on a specific piece for performance.

WEEK 4

Activities: Physical and vocal warm-up; work on monologues and duologues assignment.

This week I concentrated on looking into the subtext of the monologues I will perform. The character I am working on is troubled by the relationship he shares with his parents, and by the relationship they share with each other. In the monologue what he says has been spoken in confidence to his psychologist. This I believe will affect the way I approach the part as in this context he is being more open about his thoughts/feelings than I believe he normally would be. There are a lot of things the character; Leo is unhappy about, but at times he is trying to hide this, but his dismay and resentment still show through.

The character is considerably younger then myself so I will have to consider the best way to portray the role. When considering how I would feel if I were this character and in his circumstances I tried to recall how I would have felt about the same issues when I was of about the same age. This way I feel I can get a better understanding of why the character reacts to things the way he does. At points in the monologue he seems to have trouble staying focussed on what he's talking about and is easily distracted in his line of thought. This is probably because of his youth and because of some discomfort he feels in talking so openly.

As I am going to be playing a part younger then myself, I decided to do some observation work this week. I took my best friend's little brother to the park and watched him when he was with his friends. I observed his behaviour and how he reacted to his peers. I found it really interesting to see how he physically changed when he was with his friends to how he was when he was with me. He seemed to stand taller and had a lot more energy. He raised his voice a lot and had a lot of control over his group of friends. He was very confident, especially during a small tiff they had about a footballer. I found it really useful to do this exercise as it helped me to reflect on my character's behaviour. At various points in the monologue I have to get really angry when I am talking about my parents. I am going to make sure I consider my physicality as well as my vocal expression. I am going to stand at this point and use my arms to make my point, and then finish in a defiant pose when I have finished making my point.

WEEK 5

Activities: Physical and vocal warm up, performance with feedback on monologues and duologues for assignment.

161

Today I spent a lot of time rehearsing the duologue from 'Gasping' that Doug and I will be performing. When doing this we gave each other feedback and advice on how we could improve what we were doing and how we could interact better to improve the piece. I think we have improved since last week as we have had the chance to get used to each other's portrayal of the roles and we are able to see how we could improve further. Earlier in the week we went through the script and tried swapping characters that we read for, which I think was useful as we could see how each other would tackle the other character. This also gave us an opportunity to see our characters performed in a way that we normally wouldn't when performing them ourselves. I found that this gave me ideas on what direction I wanted to take character in, which would be very different to Doug's version of the role. I want to do the character as someone who seems quite on edge, with only fleeting moments of being fully relaxed and confident before reverting back to how he usually is. I think he would be especially like this in the context of the scene where he is dealing with his unsympathetic boss. I think this will translate well to the audience as most people will be able to relate with having to present something they are not certain about to their boss/ teacher/other authority figure. I think it's important not to play this character as too confident as I think doing so would lose any sympathy my character could get from the audience.

When we did the duologue today we received a lot of feedback about the blocking of the piece. We use a desk in it, and at times we were behind it too much so now we have made changes that bring us to the front some more. I've made notes on my copy of the script of what specific movements we make, which will help ensure we stay consistent with the physical acting. Another thing I did which I could improve on its make sure I don't rush through some parts of the dialogue. My character often lists examples to make points, and if I go through them too quickly I may be possible that the audience might not catch it all.

I also did my monologues from 'Sweet Panic' today. I did have some doubts about how I should perform the piece, but feel more confident with it now. As part of my character I portray and I find that the physical movements help me get into the mindset of the character Leo. There are some parts, which I could do more effectively which I will work on for when I have to do it again. One point in particular is when Leo is describing his mothers dancing before going on to talk about something that upsets him. I want to show that he's laughing at his mother, but not in an overly sneering way and then show the change in emotion where he gets fairly sad about what he is saying. I want to show the change in a way that seems like a natural progression and not too sudden in the change of emotion.

WEEK 6

Activities: Run-through of monologues and duologues

Today we did a run through of how we will perform our monologues and duologues for assessment next week. For the monologues the class will change between three tableaux in which each individual will perform their piece. My monologue is scheduled to happen second during the second set, although I will also be assisting Doug in a silent role during the first set. This means I am within the central focus of the staging for several minutes before my monologue and caused an unforeseen problem for me today. As part of my characterisation, my character chews gum and I didn't get an opportunity to have the gum in my mouth before I started which was how I had rehearsed it. This meant I had a little trouble speaking at the outset, but next time I'll be prepared for this and make sure it doesn't interfere with my speech. Other then this I was quite happy with how my performance went although I didn't fidget as much, which in this case was perhaps a negative as the role would have seemed better to seem more agitated.

We also went through all the duologues and I and Doug did ours which I felt went quite well. At this stage I think we know how each other are going to react and are getting better timing on our lines then we had a couple of weeks ago. One improvement I think I can make it to make some of my lines seem as if I (as the character) think I'm being ever so funny, only to then react as if I've realised my joke was failed. After we did the run through we had more time to rehearse the pieces and when I worked with Doug on the Duologue he tried the piece whilst using a makeshift fat-suit. For this character this could lead to several funny visual gags between us and some opportunities to embellish the meaning of some wording in the script to fit this. I do however have doubts whether or not this will work or simply look like a cheap visual gag and that it won't work. I cannot fully judge this until I see his full costume which he says he'll have next week.

Stanislavski Influenced Questions

Character: Leo from Sweet Panic

How old am I: Ten

What is my class? Middle

What is by breeding? I go to a decent school. Same one my Dad went to. He has not got masses of money, but has enough to give me the pocket money he does.

What am I like physically? I'm like really fast. And I'm good at football and rugby.

What am I like mentally? Really smart.

What are my strengths? I'm really clever and funny and I'm good at games and other stuff and junk.

What are my weaknesses? I hate science and my Mum is always telling me I have to tidy my room.

What do others think of me? I got loads of mates. They all think I'm great. I make 'em laugh all the time. My teacher doesn't like me, cause he has no sense of humour and is a total lame wad. My Mum and Dad think I'm a psycho or something 'cause they sent me to a shrink.

Do I know what they think? Yeah. Nuff said.

What way do I speak? English. Not like all posh or anything.

What are my personal patterns-daily routines/hobbies? I have to go to school every day, but not weekends. After school I knock for my mates Harry and Bert and Imogen. I like playing football and PS2. I'm a Grand Master at Tekken and always get and S rank. I'm not allowed out after nine so at night I just watch DVDs or if there's something good on NTL.

What is my emotional age? Mature.

What did I do last night? I had to do this project for school, I dyed my shoes purple and left them in the the sun to see if its change colour any, but it didn't. Mum was mad about that of course, but whatever.

What are my ambitions? I wanna be David Beckham. Nah just kidding. I want to be a crime scene investigator and solve all the murders and junk. Either that or be a DJ on radio 1.

What is my favourite...
   Food? Cannelloni
   Drink? Mango and Dragon fruit smoothee
   Music? Green Day
   Film? Speed

What am I doing tomorrow? I've got school, but I'll get out early 'cause I have a appointment at the chiropodists.

ASSESSOR FEEDBACK FORM

Assessment Feedback Sheet

The Imaginary High School – Music & Performing Arts Department
National Award in Performing Arts (Acting)

Learner's Name:	Daniel	**Student Number:**	70068

Assignment Title:	Monologues & Duologues

Assessor:	Kay Pringle	**Assignment Ref:**	20-MonDuo01

Date Set:	19th October	**Completion Date:**	7th December

Unit Number	Unit Title	Criteria Covered
20	Applying Acting Styles	1

Evidence for assessment complete?	YES		Is this a Final Assessment?		NO
Is this an Interim Assessment?	YES		Can the student re-submit?	YES	

Assessment

Unit	Pass				Merit		
20	P1	research a character, drawing simple conclusions about the nature of the role	✓	M1	research a character, accounting for the creative process in developing a role		✓
	Distinction				**Assessor's Comment**		
	D1	research a character, giving a comprehensive and reasoned account of the creative process and fully supporting their conclusions about the role	✓	You demonstrated an excellent understanding of the characters you played; making sure you fully justified all of your character choices in your reflective working logbook. You also made sure that you applied practitioner techniques to your development of character which you also clearly reflected on in your working logbook. Well done!		

Assessor's General Comments

Daniel, you have worked really well in this assignment. You have developed an excellent understanding of Stanislavski techniques which you constantly reflected on to help create your monologue and duologue characters. You made sure that you connected with the characters you are playing by referring back to your character work you developed during the assignment. You have made sure that you have understood the play inside-out and not just focused on your monologue and duologue parts. You need to make sure that you complete a thorough physical and vocal warm up before the assessment, so that you are focused and hold little tension in your body. At times your nerves can hold you back, you need to make sure you keep practising your breathing techniques so that you can feel confident when performing. Good luck.

Assessor's Name:	Kay Pringle
Assessor's Signature:	
Date:	7th December

Unit 54: Dance Appreciation

Assignment Sheet

The Imaginary High School
Music & Performing Arts Department
National Award in Performing Arts (Dance)

Student Name:		Student Number:	

Assignment Title:	Rambert Dance Company – Website Article

Assessor:	Ms Smith	Assignment Ref:	54-Analysis01

Date Set:	14 May	Completion Date:	14 June

Unit Number	Unit Title	Criteria Covered
54	Dance Appreciation	2, 3

Scenario

You have been approached by a dance website to watch a performance of Rambert Dance Company's current UK tour and write a critical analysis of the pieces and their creative intentions.

Grading Criteria

UNIT		Pass		Merit		Distinction
54	P2	identify the subject matter of the dance works	M2	describe the relationship between the subject matter of the dance and its context	D2	explain in detail how the context influenced the choreography
54	P3	identify the appropriateness and effectiveness of the choreographer's choice of components	M3	describe the appropriateness and effectiveness of the choreographer's structuring of components in relation to the subject matter in order to communicate meaning	D3	explain, in depth, the appropriateness and effectiveness of the choreographer's structuring of components, through a critical review of dance works using a detailed analysis

Task		Action	Criteria	Completed
1.	Observe and make notes during Rambert Dance Company's performance	• Make sure you take comprehensive notes during the performance • Research the work and/or the company further using books and/or the internet • Don't forget information within the programme	Unit 54 P2, M2, D2	
2.	Construction of article	Firstly sketch out an overall impression of your article. A good critique has the following ingredients: **1. Description** How the dance looked and sounded: space; levels; shapes; rhythm; time; dynamics; relationship in space; group design; scenic and costume design; motif & development; theme & variation **2. Analysis** Determines style and choreographer's intent: ballet; modern; jazz; tap; ethnic; combination of styles and influences; location and setting; other art forms; politics; stimuli **3. Evaluation** Effectiveness and appropriateness of choreography, how well the choreographers fulfilled their intent, and how the audience, or you, reacted and why.	Unit 54 P2, M2, D2 P3, M3, D3	
3.	Writing style	• Focus on your experience of the piece (subjective), you cannot write objectively within this article, only reflect on your perception of the work. • Limit your writing to only the most important material. • Avoid unsupported general statements. Always ensure you have explained why you came to a conclusion even if it is a personal feeling about the dancers or choreography. • Use historical or biographical context only when relevant. • Use professional vocabulary; describe male/female dancers or men/women, NOT boys/girls, guys/chicks.	Unit 54 P2, M2, D2 P3, M3, D3	
4.	Submit manuscript	Email your completed manuscript to ?????@theimaginaryhighschool.ac.uk by 1pm on 14th June.	Unit 54 P2, M2, D2 P3, M3, D3	

N.B. This assignment does not complete the assessment of this unit or the individual criteria targeted within this assignment. Students will have to successfully complete at least another two assignments during the course to meet the requirements of the unit.

UNIT 54: DANCE APPRECIATION
JACK

Devine Influence:

The first act started with two dancers on the stage, Martin the male dancer stands in front of Angela the female dancer. I thought it was not the best positioning as the more dominant male dancer should have been behind the female it would have started the dance with a greater atmosphere for me and the audience. The music starts to play which is a very fast beat composed by Beethoven called Moon Light. The dancers were then able to put together fast and snappy movements.

Both the male and female dancer wore skirts which are loose and appear to be made out of silk. The appearance of the piece would have been more influential if only the female dancer had worn a skirt and the male dancer had worn shorts, instead of clothing which made him look like he was trying to dress like a woman which then could have lead on to only the woman lifting up her dress and flapping it about. That would have made it more comical for the audience to watch and would have drawn all of the audience in especially the people who could not relate to the kind of dance that they were performing.

Enjoyment.independent.co.uk.theatre/reviews compared the dancers arm movement to pistons and how the snapped their feet. To be honest some parts of the dance made them look like monkeys. The movements are sharp and snappy which took a lot of energy from the dancers and the audience. All of the different moves they do in the dance led me to one conclusion there was far to much effort made on their account and they tried to spice it up by being cheeky which was the only thing that they could do as the music then to the dancers who were trying to keep up to it.

Transit:

This piece was a solo by Melanie Teall, performing an 8 minute solo which seem like 800. The woman was trying to recreate a moment when she looked out of her kitchen window and saw the planet Venus in transit. Strange I know? She could have thrown any moves together and still could have represented it as her experience but I have to say she did interpret it very well. The different movements that she made were very powerful she made very cool patterns sitting and lying on her front, certain parts looked as if she was being squeezed by a snake and trying to get free.

The lights and music that she used really helped the dancer show what she saw and portrayed it to us the way that she wanted. Her were many great aspects to this piece but they were all crushed to boredom that set in at about 3rd minute from there on I felt as if the dance would have been more appreciated by me if I actually knew what was actually happing at certain points, but im sure certain comments would have been noted by the dancer.

Pond way:

This piece was obviously very hard and tiring for the dancers, this piece was choreographed by Merce Cunningham in 1998, Pond ways inspiration was influenced from and exposition by Roy Lichenstein, who had a comic book approach to art. Throughout the dance there is a prominent sound of watery sounds that are echoed, which is composed by Brian Eno.

After a while it started to annoy me, the sharp and sudden movements performed by the dancers was meant to seem like wild life that would surround a pond but they obviously didn't pay enough attentionto what they were working on as no matter hard they tried it wasn't a good enough display, as they look as if they had all downed a bottle of vodka before they went on. The dancers have a weird style of dance throughout the piece as they were are all slanted at some point or another.

Stand and stare:

Stand and stare was developed by Darshan Singh Buller and self portraits by L S Lowry covered the stage. Some of the paintings were x-rayed and went really well with powerful music back fro from Bartock produced by the London Musici.

From there 19 dancers come on stage and start to entangle with each other and look like they are starting to knot together. This obviously was a complicated sequence of moves which would have been worked very hard on. Both choreographer and dancers. To be honest it looked like they were prancing around and getting themselves into a muddle and it was not until the end that you realise that they were unravelling themselves.

The weird paintings were then changed and another painting by L S Lowry came into view which was called Sea 1963. In front of this two dancers start a duet, which began to get on my nerves. The only thing that kept me watching was the pitiful sight of the 19 dancers in the background trying to make it look like they were the sea by standing and swaying.

This is not a performance that I would recommend to any of my friends as it would be w waste of money, time and evening, when they or could be watching something better at a pre-school play. As you are aware this type of performance does not interest me one bit.

ASSESSOR FEEDBACK FORM

Assessment Feedback Sheet

The Imaginary High School – Music & Performing Arts Department
National Award in Performing Arts (Dance)

Learner's Name:	Jack	Student Number:	60502

Assignment Title:	Rambert Dance Company – Website Article

Assessor:	Ms Smith	Assignment Ref:	54-Analysis01

Date Set:	14th May	Completion Date:	14th June

Unit Number	Unit Title	Criteria Covered
54	Dance Appreciation	2, 3

Evidence for assessment complete?	YES		Is this a Final Assessment?	YES	

Is this an Interim Assessment?		NO	Can the student re-submit?	YES	

Assessment

Unit		Pass			Merit	
54	P2	identify the subject matter of the dance works	✓	M2	describe the relationship between the subject matter of the dance and its context	
		Distinction			**Assessor's Comment**	
	D2	explain in detail how the context influenced the choreography			Jack, you discussed your personal feelings about this dance performance, but I do not feel you went into detail about how the pieces' choreography were influenced by the chosen stimuli. Sentences like, 'In front of this two dancers start a duet, which began to get on my nerves' do not justify your feelings with descriptive, well-informed information. Why did it get on your nerves? Perhaps some extra research into the backgrounds of this company and/or these dance pieces would benefit your written work in the future.	

Assessment

Unit		Pass			Merit	
54	P3	identify the appropriateness and effectiveness of the choreographer's choice of components	✓	M3	describe the appropriateness and effectiveness of the choreographer's structuring of components in relation to the subject matter in order to communicate meaning	
		Distinction		**Assessor's Comment**		
	D3	explain, in depth, the appropriateness and effectiveness of the choreographer's structuring of components, through a critical review of dance works using a detailed analysis		You have not spent much time evaluating the choreographic techniques used in this performance. As mentioned in your handout about writing dance critiques, you should look at space, levels, shapes, rhythm, time and dynamics. Look for interrelationships among the movement, such as: repetition and variation of the movement theme, organisation into clear sections, and the dance relationships of the dancers.		

Assessor's General Comments

It is much better now you have used you own words rather than copying from articles already on the internet. Please don't think I will not notice! If you were at university you would be in much more serious trouble. Can you please check handouts on how to use a bibliography and referencing correctly. In any kind of written work it is not appropriate to write out a website address at the beginning of a sentence. Also, you need to proof-read your own writing before handing it in. A computer will only pick up obvious spelling and grammatical errors. Read your work out loud to yourself and see if it makes sense – some of your sentence structures don't and this would be easily realised if you read your completed critique.

Although it is great to be honest about your feelings for the show, to achieve much better marks you really needed to back up your reasons more.

Assessor's Name:	Ms Smith	Student's Name:	Jack
Assessor's Signature:		Student's Signature:	
Date:	18th June	Date:	20th June

UNIT 54: DANCE APPRECIATION
NATHAN

Pond way

The dance piece called Pond way was a group piece performed by all of the thirteen female and male dancers. The choreographer of Pond way is called Merce Cunningham. Cunningham was born in April 16, 1919 in Centralia, Washington. Cunningham attended the university in Washington, Cornish school of performing and visual arts in Seattle. Cunningham was awarded the national medal of arts and membership just coming in the twentieth-century. Merce Cunningham was also in a homo-sexual relationship with a man named john cage for 54 years until Cage died in 1992. Cunningham also created his own his own dance company called Cunningham Dance Company.

Merce Cunningham's stimulus for Pond way was influenced by Roy Lichtenstein exhibition landscape in the Chinese style. Cunningham chose a backdrop of sky and water after the death of Roy Lichtenstein. Cunningham created the movements based on natural wildlife and water movements. Merce Cunningham's main stimulus for pond way was Cunningham's childhood when he used to play skimming stones. Merce Cunningham's choreography was well known for its originality and for being unpredictable. He used a lot of upper body movements of modern dance style and turn out style of ballet. Pond way's choreography involved a lot of freezes and slow and fluent movements throughout the body. There was a lot of leaps, lifts and spins in the piece. The choreography used the majority of the stage. Throughout the performance some of the dancers left the stage leaving only a handful of dancers to finish and that created a large open space used for travelling. Cunningham's piece did not project out to the audience and it did not tell a story but it did give an idea of what the dance peace is about and it dose draw you in to the performance.

The lighting throughout the piece which was created by David Covey changed by the way that it turned from lights that represented night i.e. white and black to the way that it changed when it wanted to represent Sunrise i.e. red and orange. Merce Cunningham's costume which was created by Suzanne Gallo portrayed an image of sea-gulls. The costumes were white, fitted and made with baggy parts under the arms and legs which I though represented the bird's wings. The costumes gave the dance piece much more creative looks with an outstanding effect. I thought the style of the piece was very fluent, slow and controlled. The dance used a lot of repetition and dynamics.

Throughout the whole performance there was travelling in many different directions. My personal opinion is that Merce Cunningham fulfilled his intensions towards the audience by creating a dance which gave no story line. I enjoyed the Pond way performance because of the way everything fit's i.e. the stimulus, choreography, light and costumes. The whole piece made me wonder throughout and that kept me attracted and interested to the piece. I was interested to the lighting because of the way they changed to represent sunrise and nightfall that caught my eye. The costumes made as massive impact as well. The costumes were easy to visualise and gave an idea of bird's straight away. I also was interested in the movements in the dance peace they also got a great impact from the costumes because the shapes looked more the styles of birds, fluent like water and they also added to the leaps and lifts.

Transit

The dance piece called Transit was a solo peace performed by a female dancer called Melanie Teall who also choreographed the dance piece. Melanie Teal was born in Nairobi; she trained in the arts educational school and central school of ballet and urdang academy. She was awarded the cosmopolitan C&A dance award in 1992 and the Paul Clarke award in 1993. Melanie also performed in numerous other dance companies called Charlevoise denses, Brussels and Phoenix Dance Company. Melanie joined Rambert Dance Company in 2003 and the peace of choreography for Rambert was Transit. Melanie had done some research on the planet's pathway and movement so she used this for the basic structure. Melanie's main stimulus was gravity, sculpture and the concept of infinity.

Melanie's choreography is very ordinary and simple; she uses simple front, back and side step patterns. A lot of her dances are ballet and contemporary. Melanie uses a lot of dynamics, spins, leaps and floor work and a lot of repition and syncopation in her choreography. The dance piece choreography doesn't use a lot of space mainly up & down stage there wasn't much travelling in the piece. Melanie's choreography doesn't project out to the audience and it doesn't tell me a story but it does draw you in and give you an idea of what it is about. Roland Mouret and Melanie produced a costume which portrayed an image of an ancient Egyptian warrior. This gave her performance a more creative effect. I think that the style of the dance piece is an upright upper body posture and a flexed and bendy lower body. There is a lot of walking used for travelling, syncopation, slow movements and repeated movements. The most repeated 8 counts of the dance is were the reputition is and I think that it is the main part of the dance that shows movements that brings across the idea because Melanie uses the arms and body to create a movement that looks like she is trying to keep something from inside of her from coming out and I think that is Melanie's intentions to the audience. The positioning i.e. 1st, 2nd , 3rd ... also contemporary because of all the arms and body shapes and the bendy style. Melanie's mixed these two dance styles to make a fluent and smooth dance piece.

By watching Melanie perform I felt she was portraying a message to the audience by her movements and style. I think that Melanie Teall the choreographer of Transit fulfilled her intensions to the audience by the performance and focus that was in the piece. It attracted the audience to watch and try and understand the idea that Melanie was trying to get across. Midway throughout the performance I heard the audience discussing there opinion on Melanie's idea and stimulus of the dance piece. A good positive vibe filled the theatre as Melanie performed her piece. I admired her creation of her costume; it inspired her idea of the dance. I also admired the way Melanie uses repetition of her movements to create an idea of being possessed.

ASSESSOR FEEDBACK FORM

Assessment Feedback Sheet

The Imaginary High School – Music & Performing Arts Department
National Award in Performing Arts (Dance)

Learner's Name:	Nathan	Student Number:	60430

Assignment Title:	Rambert Dance Company – Website Article

Assessor:	Ms Smith	Assignment Ref:	54-Analysis01

Date Set:	14th May	Completion Date:	14th June

Unit Number	Unit Title	Criteria Covered
54	Dance Appreciation	2, 3

Evidence for assessment complete?	YES		Is this a Final Assessment?	YES

Is this an Interim Assessment?		NO	Can the student re-submit?	YES

Assessment

Unit		Pass			Merit	
54	P2	identify the subject matter of the dance works	✓	M2	describe the relationship between the subject matter of the dance and its context	✓
		Distinction			**Assessor's Comment**	
	D2	explain in detail how the context influenced the choreography			Very good research into the background of the choreography and how this influenced the pieces	

Assessment

Unit		Pass			Merit	
54	P3	identify the appropriateness and effectiveness of the choreographer's choice of components	✓	M3	describe the appropriateness and effectiveness of the choreographer's structuring of components in relation to the subject matter in order to communicate meaning	✓
		Distinction			**Assessor's Comment**	
	D3	explain, in depth, the appropriateness and effectiveness of the choreographer's structuring of components, through a critical review of dance works using a detailed analysis		Very good ideas. Try using different words to describe different ideas (fluent, smooth used often). I liked your analysis of the choreographic techniques used and the responses you had. I also appreciated your observations of the rest of the audience, as the general 'buzz' from the audience is an important factor in whether or not the performance was successful.		

Assessor's General Comments

A good critique, demonstrating use of some research information on choreographers.

I would have liked a little more introduction of the overall evening performance, as you chose to only focus on two of the pieces.

I am glad that you decided to re-submit the article with the spelling improved. Please make sure that you get your written work checked by other people before you submit and never rely on spell checkers that can sometimes give you correct spellings but for the wrong word! You still have some errors in your work that a computer may not have been able to detect. Keep working to improve this skill.

Assessor's Name:	Ms Smith		Student's Name:	Nathan
Assessor's Signature:			Student's Signature:	
Date:	18th June		Date:	20th June

UNIT 54: DANCE APPRECIATION
SARAH

Rambert Dance Company Evaluation

On the 11th of October I had the pleasure of watching the Rambert Dance Company perform at the Wycombe Swan Theatre as part of their latest UK tour.

The performance was about two hours long, and consisted of four different dance pieces; each choreographed by different choreographers and performed by twenty two members of the dance company.

All the pieces of this performance were different in many ways and each one had a different effect on me as a viewer.

The dance that most captured my attention was the second piece called Transit, choreographed by Melanie Teall. The dance consisted of one solo female dancer, and to me created a story as I watched it. This piece was inspired by Melanie Teall seeing a sight of planet Venus in transit through her kitchen window. Her intention of the dance was to portray the pathway of space, but I had a different idea.

The visual design to me was almost like a prisoner or gladiator back in the warrior days in Italy with the Romans and the coliseums, and through the three sections of the dance we say her break free or die.

The piece started with an empty stage and blue sidelights appearing from each side of the stage and a spotlight downstage left. The dancer then slowly walked on, still with no music playing, which heightened the drama and made the viewer focus on the still dancer.

The female dancer was wearing black tight shorts, with skin coloured tights and black bands which crossed over her knees and elbows. Her top was white and looked like a bra/crop top, allowing us to see all her muscle tone in the lights. She also wore a short blonde curly wig. The crossed over bands on her elbows and knees to me resembled the armour and protection used to wear when they fought.

Throughout this performance there were three different music tracks each from Eric Serra's soundtrack to a film. The first track started, as did the dancer. To me the music sounded Egyptian, also like being in Italy, as were the Romans, which started my idea of the gladiator style.

Most of the choreography was contemporary styled and used very slow, controlled, still movement, creating an amazing effect due to the controlled movements. The dancer was very strong, as we could tell by her muscle tone, and her movements and balance throughout the piece were outstanding. She showed complete control and strong patterns and shapes in every movement. Suddenly a spotlight appeared in the centre of the stage. The music stopped and the dancer stopped in the middle of the spotlight. With both, the timing was precise. This was a great effect and caused tension as to what was going to happen next.

The accompaniment started up again, this time more dramatic and had some offbeat train sounding effects, as if she was running away from something i.e. from being prisoner or gladiator. This section involved more energy and more vigorous movements such as leaps, which showed good correlation with the music. This was almost like the climax of the piece.

Soon enough all the focus was downstage right where there was a dark, black and blue atmosphere, with a spotlight on the dancer downstage right. The music changed to a calm, softer tone, made by violins and pipes, which gave a sad, emotional feel to it. This made me think that maybe this was the section where she was set free or died and was passing on to heaven. I thought this because the spotlight was like a window to heaven, a guiding light coming down, also because the music was slow yet moving.

To me this dance was not abstract but narrative, and told an interesting story. I think this is a dance that lets your imagination roam free to think about whatever it makes you feel. The energy of the dance piece drew the audience in to the performance, instead of projecting it out. I thought the choreographer produced a really good piece, and it created a story for everyone to interpret themselves. If I thought about it relating to Venus, the actual stimulus for the piece, I can see how it would fit in with the dance; however this wasn't how I saw it.

Although this was my favourite piece out of the performance, there were also very many interesting and capturing elements during other pieces which I thought were very effective.

The first piece of the night called Devine Influence was choreographed by Martin Joyce, who said he wanted to create a piece which represented a 'beautiful dance' as set by standards of ballet.

This dance was really well performed and the movements were beautiful, but to me it didn't really have anything special or really good that made it stand out compared to the others, I though it was a bit bland.

The piece consisted of two dancers, male and female, who both wore white long stretchy, flowing skirts and the woman wore a small white crop top, but the man was bare-chested.

Most of the dance style was contemporary yet also showed lots of ballet movements throughout, which added to the intent of Martin Joyce wanting it to be 'beautiful'.

During the piece they involved using the white skirts as a prop, to perform different movements. They tugged at them, twisted them and wrapped them around each other. This gave me the idea of them being brother and sister, because as a child you often fight with your sisters and brothers and this reminded me of this and it communicated to me. As well as that, the accompaniment was a piano piece from Beethoven and it was really fast and jumpy, which weirdly reminded me of Tom and Jerry; like brother and sister, a love/hate relationship. Also the costumes portray innocence as they were white, almost like purity, just like young children.

I think the choreographer definitely succeeded in producing a 'beautiful dance' because all the movements were mainly smooth, continuous and really controlled.

Similarly to this, the third piece of the night called Pond Way, choreographed by Merce Cunningham wasn't abstract either, it was based on events, not a story.

The stimulus for this dance was the paintings of the famous pop artist Roy Lichtenstein. For the dance, Merce Cunningham chose a picture of sky and water to be enlarged as a backdrop resembling the dance images of wildlife and water movement, and memories of skimming stones as a child.

The backdrop was blue with a large grey shape almost like a whale shape taking up the top half of the picture. This collaborated with the music, which was very eerie and had whale like sounds all the way through, giving a sense of being underwater. In the bottom left corner there was also a small boat, giving me an idea of the sea. This backdrop was very interesting and helped the audience get a feel of the underwater theme.

The dance consisted of about 15 dancers, all in white stretchy long trousers and stretchy baggy long sleeved tops. I feel that the costume was baggy to give a flowing look and to give free movement, just like fish who are entirely free and can move in any way or where they want. To me the dancers were the tiny fish around this whale, which was also emphasised by the fact there were a lot of dancers on stage.

The lighting was very good in this piece and captured my attention well. From the left the sidelights were blue, and from the right the colours were orange. I felt this represented the colours under the sea e.g. coral.

The style was contemporary and had good complexity and timing throughout. The dance used a lot of canon in it, which was very effective and reminded me of the waves in the sea. This whole piece made me feel calm and relaxed because of the accompaniment and the movements used.

I think the choreographer used interesting movements to demonstrate the feeling of water and its movement. Although my idea of this dance isn't actually what the intent was, I thought it used really good costumes, lighting and design to show the intent of the piece.

In contrast to all of these pieces, the forth and last piece of the night was entirely abstract and very different to all the others. Stand and Stare is the name of the piece, and it was choreographed by Darshan Singh Buller.

His approach to choreographing this piece was to portray the emotions behind Lowry's paintings. Lowry's paintings were usually on canvasses and made up of layers of images on top of each other, resulting in resembling memories.

In this dance piece there were four large paintings, placed in different positions on stage and hanging from above. They were all vertical and quite narrow. You couldn't really tell what each picture was of or about. They were all really dull and consisted of colours such as grey, black and brown.

I could pick out one image at least on each picture, i.e. an eye or a nose, but they were just images on top of one another.

These pictures were very unordinary and very different to what you would usually see in a dance piece, that is why I liked it and found it interesting, because it's not something you would usually expect to see.

The dance was like this from the beginning to the end.

To start off, the music was very random with no counts. There were unusual outbreaks of loud crashes, and the accompaniment was mostly piano.

The movements were contemporary styled and it was amazing how in time all the dancers were because the music was very hard to dance to. It was as if they had to guess when to do the next movement because the music wasn't giving the beats away easily.

Throughout the dance a lot of repetition was used especially arm movements. To me this resembled the whole idea of memories. The dance overall didn't really mean much to me or communicate anything to me because it was completely abstract. It didn't really make me feel anything other than confusion throughout it.

Even though it was an abstract piece, there was a lot of really interesting elements to it that I found effective.

At one stage, all of the lights snapped off, and this was juxtaposition to the bright white light we had been seeing beforehand. As the lights turned off a few dancers ran on stage, then the lights turned on and then snapped off again, a few more dancers ran on, and this carried on. I found this effective because it took a while for your eyes to adjust to the lighting, so you didn't really notice the dancers running on, and it seemed as if the dancers had magically appeared.

I also enjoyed it when all the giant pictures started to move, some lifted up, some just moved from left to right continuously. I found it effective simply because it was out of the blue and it added to the whole abstract style. During the piece, the accompaniment was forever changing tempo and the lighting was always changing. I think this was good because it had a lot of variety to make the dance more interesting, seeing as this dance piece was very long.

This dance piece used a bit of everything i.e. canon, unison, repetition, music change, lighting change, lots of lifts and contact work, interesting background images and pictures etc... which made it exciting to watch.

Overall I loved the show even though I found some pieces a bit bland and felt they dragged on a little bit. However there were a few pieces I found exciting to watch and think about. I think choreographers fulfilled their intent on their pieces and each one of them produced a very successful dance.

180

ASSESSOR FEEDBACK FORM

Assessment Feedback Sheet

The Imaginary High School – Music & Performing Arts Department
National Award in Performing Arts (Dance)

Learner's Name:	Sarah	Student Number:	60434

Assignment Title:	Rambert Dance Company – Website Article

Assessor:	Ms Smith	Assignment Ref:	54-Analysis01

Date Set:	14th May	Completion Date:	14th June

Unit Number	Unit Title	Criteria Covered
54	Dance Appreciation	2, 3

Evidence for assessment complete?	YES		Is this a Final Assessment?	YES

Is this an Interim Assessment?		NO	Can the student re-submit?	YES

Assessment

Unit		Pass			Merit	
54	P2	identify the subject matter of the dance works	✓	M2	describe the relationship between the subject matter of the dance and its context	✓
		Distinction			**Assessor's Comment**	
	D2	explain in detail how the context influenced the choreography	✓	You clearly identified the influences on the choreographer and I enjoyed insight into your interpretation of their work		

Assessment

Unit		Pass			Merit	
54	P3	identify the appropriateness and effectiveness of the choreographer's choice of components	✓	M3	describe the appropriateness and effectiveness of the choreographer's structuring of components in relation to the subject matter in order to communicate meaning	✓
		Distinction			**Assessor's Comment**	
	D3	explain, in depth, the appropriateness and effectiveness of the choreographer's structuring of components, through a critical review of dance works using a detailed analysis	✓		A well thought-out critique. Good insights and analysis skills demonstrated	

Assessor's General Comments

Well done Sarah. I really enjoyed your evaluation. You had some very good insights and I can really see that you put a lot of thought into your ideas. I'm so glad this performance opened some new doors for you.

I've made some grammatical corrections – ways to be more direct with your writing style. Active voice rather than passive. You sometimes have a tendency to repeat yourself at the beginning and end of sentences, which isn't needed. Have a look at these comments and use this for next time.

Assessor's Name:	Ms Smith	Student's Name:	Sarah
Assessor's Signature:		Student's Signature:	
Date:	18th June	Date:	20th June